The Life and Times of Dundee

CHRISTOPHER A. WHATLEY
DAVID B. SWINFEN
ANNETTE M. SMITH

JOHN DONALD PUBLISHERS LTD
EDINBURGH

ISBN 0 85976 388 9

British Library Cataloguing in Publication Data
A catalogue record for this book is available from the
British Library.

Phototypeset by ROM-Data Corporation Ltd, Falmouth,
Cornwall, England.
Printed & bound in Great Britain by J. W. Arrowsmith
Ltd, Bristol

Contents

Acknowledgements

Our first debt is to John Tuckwell, formerly of John Donald Ltd, who over a 'peh', chips and beans and a pint in the Phoenix Bar in the Nethergate, first suggested that this book should be written. Russell Walker has revived what at one time was an ailing project and with firm but graceful professionalism has seen it to completion. Along with the publishers we are extremely grateful too to the Carnegie Trust for awarding us a generous grant towards the cost of reproducing the illustrations.

The lonely and often dispiriting task of writing has been lightened by the cheerful and enthusiastic assistance we have had from those individuals we have pestered for sources, information and illustrations at times when we periodically broke free from the chains of our word processors. Chief amongst these have been Iain Flett and Richard Cullen of the Dundee District Archive and Record Centre, Robert N. Smart and Christine Gascoigne of St Andrews University Archives, Joan Auld and the staff of Dundee University Archives, Anna Robertson of Dundee Museums and Art Galleries, Linda McGill and the staff of the Local History Section, Dundee District Libraries and Steve Connolly of Perth and Kinross District Archives. Janice Murray and in particular David Stockdale of Dundee Museums went out of their way both to find and provide us with descriptions of suitable illustrative material. Douglas Spence and his staff at D.C. Thomson & Co. kindly sought out illustrations for us from his company's extensive photographic archive. Our sincere thanks are due to the institutions and bodies concerned for granting us permission to reproduce illustrations from their collections. The map showing the outline of the medieval town was kindly and expeditiously drawn by Jimmy Ford of the Department of Geography, University of Dundee.

Each of us has benefited from discussions on various occasions over the years about the history of Dundee with a number of individuals. Elizabeth P. D. Torrie, Enid Gauldie, Veronica Smart and William M. Walker spring immediately to mind. Also influential in different ways were Billy Kay, Graham R. Smith, Elizabeth McGrath, John M. Frew,

Eleanor Gordon, Leah Leneman, Christopher Smout and our colleagues in the departments of Scottish History in the University of St Andrews and Modern History in the University of Dundee. Participants at conferences and evening classes in local history run by the Centre for Tayside and Fife Studies and the Continuing Education Department at the University of Dundee have often unwittingly provided information, as well as warnings (which we have heeded but too often we fear ignored) that it is impossible to get inside the history of Dundee from written sources alone.

We are grateful to H. A. Whatley for his painstaking work in constructing the index.

Finally we should thank respectively one partner, Pat, one wife, Ann, and one husband, Alex, for their forbearance and support during the writing of the book. Between them they made the going much smoother than we had a right to expect it to be.

Dundee, 1993

C.A.W
D.B.S.
A.M.S.

Illustrations

Introduction

Few towns in Scotland can have been so misrepresented or misunderstood as Dundee. By identifying it with William McGonagall and cartoon characters such as 'Oor Wullie', and the first, failed, Tay rail bridge, it is easy to portray it as a slightly ridiculous, tragi-comic place. Its association with coarse and often dowdy jute cloth, its legendary nineteenth century poverty, and its sometimes hard-faced women have created in the popular mind the image of a depressed and forbidding urban centre, somewhere to leave out of a tour itinerary in favour of nearby 'historic' St Andrews. The phrase 'Jute, Jam and Journalism' easily trips off the tongue during casual discussion in which Dundee is mentioned. Like all impressions, these have some basis in reality. There is much more to Dundee however, which it is the purpose of this book to demonstrate.

Dundee is one of Scotland's oldest towns, and in 1991 celebrated the octocentenary of the probable granting of its burghal status, around 1191. Even before that however there was a 'shire' of Dundee, which indicates that it was already a centre of some importance. In the middle ages the burgh was one of the four greatest in the land, its church, St Mary's, richly-endowed and in appearance one of the finest north of the border. By the sixteenth century Dundee was second only to Edinburgh in Scotland's economic league, with a range of trading connections throughout northern Europe, dealing not only in raw materials but also manufactures such as woollen and (significantly) 'Lynnen' cloth.

Culturally the burgh was very much in the mainstream of European development. One of its most eminent citizens, Hector Boece, who was educated at the High School, later became acquainted with Erasmus and other major scholars of his day, and wrote one of the earliest histories of Scotland. The three Wedderburn brothers, John, James and Robert, sons of a Dundee merchant, each wrote and published during their lifetimes, although it was John who was largely responsible for the *The Gude and Godlie Ballads*, a remarkable collection which in poetic form brought the teaching of the early Reformation directly into educated Scottish hands. With the addition of George Wishart's preaching and the anti-papist plays

1

of Robert Wedderburn, Dundee's vicar, as well as the burgh's associations with Knox, Dundee could with some justification be described as the 'second Geneva'.

The seventeenth century was a less propitious time for Dundee, and indeed while things improved in the eighteenth too there was little sign that it would be able to recapture its former prosperity in trade, grandeur in building or reputation for its literature—although like Boece, the poet Robert Fergusson did attend the High School.

In the nineteenth century however Dundee rose once more, this time as 'Juteopolis', the world's jute capital, with its cloth being shipped to all four corners of the globe, the city integrated into a worldwide network which began with the annual jute crops of the Bengali ryots (or smallholders) and ended on the prairies and ranches of North America, opened up in part with the profits of Dundee jute manufacturers. In the long run however this was a mixed blessing, as the economics of the industry in the age of 'laissez-faire' produced human suffering and physical deterioration in Dundee which has only been eradicated in the half century since the Second World War. Nevertheless the Victorian era was an enormously productive one for Dundee, not only in textiles, but in engineering, mill and factory building, shipbuilding—as well as architecture and the arts, in ways which are often overlooked. For example, small-scale printing and bookselling—along with working class writing—thrived in a town which is better known for the squalor of its housing, drunkenness and other social evils. One of those small proprietors, with premises in Castle St, was James Chalmers, now widely recognised as the inventor of the postage stamp.

The process of disengagement from jute was long drawn out, and indeed it is really only in the past two decades that the beating of Dundee's economic and social pulse has ceased to depend on that trade. Now Dundee addresses the world as the 'City of Discovery', a slogan which is by no means unwarranted. While the book ends on a positive note, this is not to suggest that modern-day Dundee has rid itself of all of its ills. The worst housing has been swept away, but there are still pockets of poverty and decay. There have been failures and disappointments too, such as the city's inability to attract as much North Sea oil-related business as was hoped. Riverside, on the north bank of the Tay, potentially one of the most beautiful walkways in the country, lies half and inappropriately developed, testimony to misplaced planning and the effects of the current recession. Because of this, like much of the rest of Britain, Dundee suffers from too high a level of unemployment and attendant social problems such as poverty, drug abuse, a high illegitimacy rate and apparently mindless vandalism. Even so, Dundee has been transformed, for the better. The nature of that considerable achievement will become clearer to those who read this book.

Part of the process of rebuilding and rediscovery has been a growing interest in the city's past, more professional and serious research and consequentially a healthy stream of historical publications. Some of these have been good, a few excellent. Others have been trite. Usually the best have dealt with specific aspects of the city's history over relatively short periods of time—women workers in the nineteenth century, trade unions in the later Victorian and Edwardian eras, the modern textile industry and industrial archaeology. A brief 'Further Reading' section has been included at the end of the book as a guide to what we have judged the most useful and relevant works.

There is a gap however which this book hopes to fill. It provides a much-needed general account of Dundee's history from the time of the earliest written records—the twelfth century—to the present day. It also covers a wide range of integrated topics. It has been profusely illustrated. The hope is that it will provide a coherent and rounded introduction to the city's history which can be read or simply looked at by Dundonians or visitors to the city or indeed anyone with more than a passing interest in Dundee. Although many may heave a sigh of relief that we have not had recourse to the usual scholarly apparatus of footnotes, all readers can be assured that two linked objectives have been borne in mind at all times: first, that what was written should be based on the most authoritative modern accounts, and second, that it should be readable and comprehensible to the non-specialist.

That the book has been written by three authors may raise fears that it is yet another disparate collection of essays, at least two of which have appeared in recent years. It is true that each of us has concentrated on a particular aspect of Dundee's history: Annette Smith on the medieval period, Christopher Whatley on economic and social history, and David Swinfen on ships, the sea and politics. Considerable effort however has gone into editing the book and merging the contributions in the hope that the joins will hardly be discernible.

We are none of us are natives of Dundee—two are Fifers and one comes from the West of Scotland—but we have all worked here for many years. We have grown to love and respect the place, and accordingly, this book is dedicated to the citizens—past and present—of a remarkable town.

Part I
Beginnings and Medieval Dundee

CHAPTER 1

The Founding and the Growth of the Town

The Earliest Settlement

A 'Life and Times' might be expected to begin by giving the parentage and date of birth of the subject. In the case of Dundee this is difficult. Geologists can explain the movements on the earth's surface million of years ago which have helped to make the scenery and physical surroundings of Dundee so striking. Archaeologists have discovered sure signs that soon after the glaciers of the Ice Age retreated between BC 8000 and 9000 human beings settled in Fife and north of the Tay, at the Stannergate for instance.

There has been fairly continuous human habitation in Fife and Tayside since then. From the historians of Rome and the old chroniclers we learn that the Romans knew the Carse of Gowrie, camped at Longforgan and probably marched along the fertile Strathmore valley. Later the Picts and Scots fought out their obscure battles in the plains and mountains behind the Sidlaws. The Vikings may have sailed along the Tay as far as Perth.

What historians do not know is where the first Dundonians came from. Who were the settlers were who first made their homes on the land that is now known as the Seagate, between the Scouringburn and Dens burns? This was the beginning of what we now call Dundee and it is believed that the first settlement there can be dated at some point in the eleventh century.

Sometimes a name helps historical research. There have been various interpretations of 'Dundee'. The spelling has varied, becoming fixed in its modern form only in the nineteenth century. One version, Dondie, was believed to be a corruption of the Latin *Donum Dei*, Gift of God. Hector Boece (c.1465—1536), the first principal of Aberdeen University, was born near the town and he claimed that it was at one time called *Alectum*, beautiful place. But Boece was a somewhat unreliable historian and his seems to be the only evidence for this.

W. F. H. Nicolaisen, today's foremost scholar in the study of place names, has suggested somewhat hesitantly that as the Gaelic for Dundee is *Dun Deagh*, the derivation may be Fort (Dun) of Diag, a Celtic man's name meaning fire. This could mean that Gaelic speaking Celts were in the area and lived in a hill-fort on Dundee Law until more secure conditions allowed them to move down to the coast. This process had happened in other areas, but we cannot be sure. It could be that a colony simply moved along from the Stannergate.

Whatever the circumstances, these early settlers chose a good place. There was plenty of fresh water from two burns, which then reached the river about quarter of a mile from each other but were diverted during the building of the modern industrial town and are now culverted over. Small hills to the west, Corbie and Castle, provided some shelter from the prevailing west wind while small boats dragged up on to the shore gained protection from the scour of the Tay from Castle Rock and St Nicholas Craig. Corbie, lying behind what is now the Overgate, was excavated during the modern extension of the town.

The original coast line has long disappeared as the town extended into the Tay on reclaimed land, but the name Castle Street commemorates the rock and the castle believed to stand there while St Nicholas Craig is also hidden, partly under British Rail's Taybridge station.

The soil in the area was fertile, and the fish from the Tay provided a ready source of food. The site was also in a very favourable geographical situation to take advantage of the economic conditions which arose in the twelfth century. This was a period of rising population and rural prosperity when all over Western Europe towns began to appear as centres of trade, for the exchange and sale of agricultural produce. With local ferry and international sea-routes easily accessible, a sheltered harbour and produce for trading available from Fife, from the hinterland in Angus, and from the sea, Dundee could not have been better situated.

Dundee and Earl David

Apparently the settlement was already prosperous enough to be regularly visited by the travelling courts of the eleventh century, though the tradition that King Edgar lived and died there in 1107 is now questioned. The historian is on more certain ground in the second half of the twelfth century when the name 'Dundeeshire' makes its first appearance in written documents. This defined an area in the hinterland of what is now the city of Dundee and shows that it was by that time important enough or conveniently enough situated to be considered the administrative centre.

One of the earliest known maps of Scotland, drawn by Matthew of Paris, a monk at St Albans, probably about 1250. Dundee is in its exact geographical position, and one of the few names in Scotland, showing that the town was already significant.

However prosperous it may have been previously, the small port's commercial development was undoubtedly accelerated by its association with David, Earl of Huntingdon, brother and for a time heir of King

William the Lion. The king was seeking to consolidate his power in the north of Scotland and employed his brother as his main agent. Between 1178 and 1182 Earl David was granted lands on both sides of the Tay, including Dundee.

It has been alleged that William's grant was a mark of his thankfulness for his brother's safe return from a Crusade but there seems to be no historical proof that David ever took part in such a venture. There is no doubt however that he helped William to govern, and his control over large areas of Scotland, including Dundee, was part of this process.

David was also a powerful English lord, acquiring the title by which he is best known from the lordship of Huntingdon. In 1199, through his position at the English court and his relationship with the English king, John, he obtained considerable trading privileges for the benefit of what from about 1190 he was calling 'my burgh'. The agreement allowed traders from Dundee to deal with all English ports except London without paying the usual customs and dues and also granted trading concessions in parts of France under English control.

He also encouraged new settlers. Robert Furmage for instance received the gift of a 'toft' of land. Some of these new inhabitants may have been English or Anglo-French, but some Scots may have adopted foreign names. Earl David's officials in the burgh were certainly not Scots. The clerk, Philip and the constable, Saer de Tenys, were brought in to administer the Scottish lands just as David's large estates in England were managed. The earl's interest in this was that if the burgh's wealth increased so did his rents.

The Castle of Dundee

As King William's main reason for infefting his brother with the burgh was to maintain order, it is possible that the castle of Dundee was built at this time. The castle's history is obscure. During the Wars of Independence a large fortification undoubtedly existed, sometimes in English sometimes in Scottish hands, but it disappears from the records thereafter, leaving only its name in Castle Rock, Castle Wynd of the thirteenth century and now Castle Street.

It is not inconceivable that Robert the Bruce ordered its demolition after it was finally captured by the Scots. This was a policy he followed successfully all over Scotland, thereby depriving the English army of possible refuges and future bases for attacking his forces.

But the burgh's growth did not depend wholly on its military status and was not hampered by the death of its patron David in 1219. When Mathew Paris drew a map of Scotland in the middle of the thirteenth century Dundee was one of the few names appearing on it, showing that it was known in England and Europe, no doubt through its traders. It would already be a busy bustling little port where foreign sailors, traders and ships from France, Holland, England and Scandinavia were a common sight and foreign tongues were commonly heard.

The settlement had begun to extend westward, and there were a few tenements in the Flukergait, later the Nethergate, even before Earl David obtained the superiority of the burgh. The attraction to the west may have been the better safer anchorage to be found in the small bay between the Castle Rock and St Nicholas Craig, which was sheltered from every wind but the south and could also cater for larger boats.

The Seagate however remained the administrative centre for some time. When Robert I gave permission for a tolbooth to be built the Seagate was still the chosen site and the Market Cross stood there in the late thirteenth century. But the feeling of security engendered by the very existence of the castle would encourage new building nestling round it and the presence of the church of St Clement's in that area probably shows too that the commercial heart of the settlement moved west quite early in the burgh's history.

Some indication of how far the town had spread by the end of the twelfth century is given by the first name of the church which Earl David may have founded, St Mary's in the Field. It was the late fifteenth century before buildings in the Overgate and Nethergate spread much to the west of the church despite the buildings known to have existed in the Flukergait in the twelfth century, notably Earl David's residence, which may have stood just opposite it.

Though the Seagate kept its population the loss of its earlier importance was marked by the removal of the tolbooth to the Marketgate from the site given by the king in 1325, a site still marked by a wall tablet. It is likely that the move took place soon after the setting up of the tron about 1363 in the west end of the Marketgate, near the north end of present-day Crichton Street. The tron was the beam used for weighing goods publicly and the tolbooth was the meeting place for burgh courts and council, for collecting tolls and customs. It made sense to have all that was necessary for business gradually accumulated in that area of the town, near the harbour from which so much of the burgh's wealth flowed. The Market Cross was eventually moved there too.

The Mercat Cross was erected in 1586, but removed in 1777 from the west end of High Street as it obstructed traffic. The Cross was very important in the early burgh as the centre of economic and administrative life. The lower tower was used for meetings and public proclamations were made from its flat roof. The present cross is made up of bits of the old cross that have survived.

Further Expansion

Expansion north was limited by geological conditions until modern times when more advanced technology helped overcome these. For instance, the dolerite outcrop, Corbie hill, provided some shelter but also prevented expansion north, as did the swampy ground, the Meadows, which stretched from the present day Ward Road to the Wellgate.

These physical restrictions meant that building spread on raised beaches from the Marketgate, now the High Street, along the Nethergate and Argyll or Overgate, the lower and upper roads to the west, while the Seagate, the Murraygate and to a smaller extent the Cowgate were developed to the east. By the late fifteenth century not only the street fronts were largely filled up; in some of the backlands there was housing for the less well-off to provide for the expanding population and also perhaps industrial building. That process continued and intensified so that there was eventually great congestion in the vennels and closes running between the larger houses facing the main streets.

There were still open spaces, however, on the street fronts and behind houses, for town and country were not totally separated for many centuries. Gardens and orchards were attached to the spacious houses of people like the earl Crawford, whose house and grounds ran from the Nethergate to the river. Small men too had their ground within the burgh, as we know from the complaint made to the burgh court by Alexander Paterson when some French soldiers jumped the dyke into his garden and stole his kale in February 1552.

Even in the eighteenth century there was some open ground surrounded by hedges in the Overgate. And always there were gap sites where houses had been destroyed by fire, by enemy action or had simply been allowed to fall into disrepair by their owners. It is interesting however that Dundee though deliberately set on fire by the English army in 1548 never experienced the great accidental fires that almost destroyed so many other burghs, notably Glasgow.

Physical Changes in the Town

Over the centuries the appearance of the burgh was to change quite dramatically. The first houses in the Seagate would have been little more than huts made of wattle, with roofs perhaps of heather thatching or turf. By the thirteenth century many were sturdier, depending on a more solidly based frame, but still largely made of wood. As the town and at least some of its inhabitants grew wealthier, while nobles like Earl Crawford and local gentry also built their town houses there, quite grand houses appeared and by the end of the sixteenth century stone was increasingly used for some of these.

Of course, the dwellings squeezed into the backlands to accommodate the poorer members of the community would be more ramshackle, perhaps still only wood and wattle shacks. Some larger public buildings would be of stone, notably the churches, but little remains of buildings public or private of early Dundee and too much has been lost comparatively recently. For instance 'Woodenlands', an early sixteenth century house, was destroyed only in 1876, while the distinctive old turreted house which stood facing into High Street at the end of the Overgate, General Monck's headquarters in 1651, was demolished with the old Overgate, to be replaced by a chain store and shopping precinct in the 1960s.

The original street plan, compared by one commentator to a man lying with his limbs stretched out from his body—the Marketgate, now High Street—is still the basis of the centre of the modern city, though the street levels have gradually become much higher. Unfortunately buildings erected within the burgh before 1700 which might have helped to illustrate the town's history can be counted on the fingers of one hand.

Gardyne's House, 70-73 High Street, of late sixteenth century construction, is completely hidden from the street. Though on each road giving entrance to the town there were ports, probably eventually of stone, or barrasses—barricades mostly of wood—the Cowgate port alone survives, largely because it was believed that it was from it that the Reformer, George Wishart preached. However, it was probably built in 1592 long after Wishart's death.

All traders entering or leaving the town had to pass through these ports with their goods so that they could not evade the town's customs. The gates would be shut at night to prevent illegal entry of goods and also to act as the first line of defence in troubled times. The ports were moved to different positions at various times to accommodate the growth of the town and were all except that in the Cowgate removed about 1770.

Early Churches

Fortunately the impressive Old or St Mary's Steeple still dominates the area between the Overgate and the Nethergate. While the steeple dates only from the late fifteenth century there had been churches there before, also dedicated to the Virgin Mary, St Mary's in the Field. Several times English invaders destroyed or damaged whatever stood there and then the civil wars of the seventeenth century also resulted in severe damage.

Two churches were associated with Dundee by the middle of the thirteenth century, St Mary's and St Clement's, but it is not certain when either was built. Hector Boece tells the story that David, earl of Huntingdon, built a church in Dundee in thanks for safe return from the Crusades. It will be remembered that William the Lion is credited with giving David land for the same reason. There can be doubts about why David established a church but it seems certain that he did have one built.

Gardyne's house in Gray's or Kyd's close. Still in existence but very unfortunately hidden from view, this is a splendid example of a sixteenth-century Dundee burgess house. John Gardyne, mariner burgess and his wife were the first recorded owners in 1560. It originally was decorated with painted ceilings, typical of houses of the well-to-do in late sixteenth and early seventeenth century Scotland.

Though there are also some doubts as to whether the church he gave to the monks of Lindores was St Mary's or St Clement's, the chances are that it was St Mary's, as the burgh took over its maintenance from the Lindores abbot in 1442/3.

At that time burgh pride all over Scotland was high, and there was dissatisfaction in Dundee with the way the church had been maintained. The town council had it repaired and extended and by the end of the fifteenth century the structure was complete. It was one of the largest parish churches in Scotland at the time and today it boasts the 'highest surviving medieval ecclesiastical tower' in the country.

Internally it was gradually beautified and lavishly decorated by endowments of perhaps 35 altars with their associated chaplains. Wealthy families like the Spaldings and organisations such as the Guildry and the craft incorporations all gave money to the church for this purpose. Unfortunately its glory was shortlived, as we shall see in a later chapter.

St Clement's, which lay near the castle in the midst of the most heavily populated part of the burgh, may had been the original parish church. With its churchyard which ran down to the harbour it initially occupied much of the ground where the Caird Hall and Square now stand. Most Dundonians were buried in the yard or within the churches themselves until in 1564 Queen Mary donated the Howff to the town as a burial ground. St. Clement's churchyard was overcrowded, thus it was believed giving rise to 'pest' and other contagious diseases.

What part St Clement's later played in town worship is not certain but in the second half of the sixteenth century secular buildings were encroaching on the churchyard, notably a new grammar school and a tolbooth. The church seems to have fallen into in a bad state of repair and part of its site was used as a weigh-house for storage of the tron and the standard weights.

It is possible that the chapels in various places around the town were also built of stone. Only six can be proved to have existed, rather fewer than has sometimes been claimed. The use of rents to endow altars in St Mary's may have led to the transferring of the name of the saint to whom the altar was dedicated to the land that was the source of its income. The belief that an even older church called St Paul's existed between the Murraygate and the Seagate probably arises from such confusion.

But there were also two friaries and a least one nunnery. The Howff was part of the gardens of the Franciscans in whose church the clergy recognised Robert the Bruce as king in 1314 or 1315. As the Greyfriars usually established themselves outside town boundaries, this demonstrates the limits of the burgh at the time. The Dominicans, the Blackfriars, were not established in Dundee until just after 1517 when they too built a friary just beyond the burgh bounds on the west of the town, perhaps between the Overgate and Nethergate ports.

Both houses were to disappear during the religious changes of the middle of the sixteenth century. The Franciscan friary may have been burned during the English attack in 1548 but its ruin was completed after 1560 when the town council ordered that the kirk and

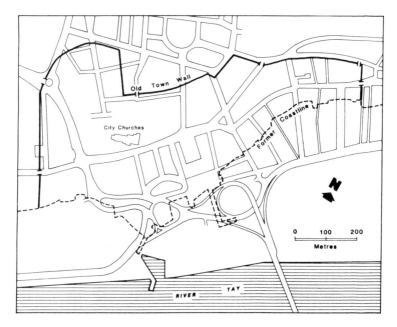

Map showing the line of the burgh wall and the original shore line superimposed on the modern street plan which may help readers understand the growth of the town.

steeple of the Greyfriars should be used for the 'common weil' of the town. Stones removed from Blackfriars may have helped strengthen the harbour. The small Franciscan nunnery established in 1501/2 had also gone by 1560.

Dundee's physical appearance then has never been static, as we can gather from the changing use of some of its buildings and the disappearance of so many others. In medieval and early modern times until the seventeenth century the picture we are given by contemporaries is of a very attractive town. It managed to recover from the ravages of invaders surprisingly well. Of course, wooden buildings were easy to rebuild but the town's pride in itself ensured that its public buildings did not lie in ruins for too long.

The Burgh Wall

Even though town walls were not usual in Scotland in medieval times, it is perhaps surprising to find that there was no protective wall round

Dundee until quite late in its history. The burgh sat on an obvious entry to the heart of the country, the Tay, and it was fiercely attacked by invaders on several occasions. It has been claimed both that the English tried to improve the defences of the town and that a wall was begun by the French soldiers in the pay of Mary of Guise. Most recent archaeological evidence tells a different story, while the town council's order to the townspeople in 1582 to make sure their back dykes were in good repair and the back yetts (gates) shut at night seems to indicate that back garden walls alone provided the town's first line of defence.

In 1591 royal permission was granted to build a town wall, which was constructed under the supervision of William Duncan in 1592. Strengthened in the 1640s it seems to have used the garden walls already in existence. Its line can be seen in the map on p. 16. It was not strong enough to keep out either Montrose in 1645 or Monck in 1651: their armies did more lasting damage to the town than any previous marauders. However, to judge from the engravings by John Slezer made in the 1680s the general appearance of the burgh did not change drastically then, though individual buildings as well as the population suffered quite badly.

The Early Harbour

One constant feature in Dundee life has been the sea and the importance of the harbour reflects this. In the early town, the Tay would always be in view—over Earl Crawford's garden, through some of the narrow vennels leading down to the shore from the main thoroughfares, from St Clement's churchyard.

The first 'harbour' was simply a sheltered beach, which because of the position of the settlement was secured from every wind except the south. We do not know when the first pier was built and despite the importance of sea trade to the town, its inhabitants were slow to develop a sophisticated approach to its upkeep. It was 1447 before any record can be found of official steps to finance maintenance and any improvements of the harbour. On 10 July in that year James II granted letters patent to the Town Council permitting them to set up a schedule of shore dues on goods coming into the port. There was a charge to freemen of 'the king's burghs' of 2d and to unfreemen of 4d on every serplare (80 stones) of wool and skins brought in. On every chalder (about 96 bushels) of corn, malt or salt, freemen had to pay 2d, the unfree 4d.

Vessels paid according to their size but despite the recognition of the

Council's responsibility for the harbour, it was 1612 before a register of all ships was instituted, with a fine of £5 Scots imposed on masters who neglected their duty in this respect.

From 1447 onwards there are regular references in the Town Council minutes to harbour repairs and regulations concerning the behaviour of those using it. In 1458 the 'haven silver' was appropriated from vessels coming in for repair. A century later a piermaster was appointed because the 'shoar bulwark and haven had been so little regardit this long tyme bygone' that it was felt it could shortly 'decay and come to ruin' and this official, a member of the Town Council, had also to handle the harbour finances. In 1644 the Council provided another amenity for traders, a packhouse for the storage of goods.

One aspect of municipal control was that all interests in the burgh had to be considered. When one pier was shown to be damaging the salmon fishing, it had to be taken down. The pier seems to have been mostly masonry but as the bulwarks were wooden it was forbidden to heat pitch near it. In the late sixteenth century a wright, probably a worker in wood, George Black, was in charge. He did not give satisfaction, however, and was replaced by Thomas Waill.

Waill and his successors seem to have been better at the job of filling in the bulwarks with ballast for it was 1647 before there was further mention of weakness there. In 1668 James Anderson, shoremaster, was commissioned by the Town Council to freight a ship for Norway to bring a load of oak trees for backing and repairing the bulwarks where they were 'most decayit'. Ships that damaged these or any other part of the 'shore', as the harbour was called, were supposed to be responsible for any necessary repairs and in 1669, Thomas Bower was instructed to 'use all possible diligence' to repair the damage done by his ship.

Rules were also made to ensure orderly management of business at the harbour. Obstreperous behaviour such as 'drawing a whinger' (a short sword) or 'giving a cuff' was fined £5 Scots. Empty ships were expected to move away from the quay so that others could load and unload; there was to be no loading or handling of tackle during the night between one hour after sunset and one hour before sunrise and any goods so handled could be confiscated.

While it was sensible to insist that the quays were to be kept free of obstructions, for centuries little attention was paid to making similar rules about access to these quays. In 1562 Skirling's, later Tyndal's wynd was one of the two principal passages to the harbour. Yet the houseowners there, including David Gardiner, who was himself a mariner and might have been expected to realise the importance of a clear road to the ships, were allowed to build out into the lane. As a result there was room for only a pack horse to pass through the wynd. Access improved only in the late eighteenth century when new roads such as Crichton Street were built.

The Tay Ferries

The Town Council also had control over the various ferries across the Tay to Fife. In 1641 the Duke of Lennox, Admiral of the Scottish fleet, conferred on the magistrates the office of 'Admiraltie' over the river. This gave them power to summon all boatmen and ferrymen on both sides of the Tay to fix dues and make regulations as they thought suitable. In 1595 Patrick Kinnaird of that Ilk obtained a charter from the Scottish Privy Council granting him rights over 'all and haill the passage of the water of Tay at Dundee' but the burgesses of the town were not prepared to admit this right and managed to keep control in Dundee hands.

Guid Gear in Small Bulk

By the middle of the seventeenth century we can see that Earl David's burgh was a thriving urban centre. Despite being hemmed in by river, hills and swamps its population grew steadily particularly at the end of the sixteenth and the beginning of the seventeenth centuries. One informed 'guestimate' for the numbers in 1645 is 11,200. Natural increase obviously accounted for some of this but a settlement as prosperous as Dundee was bound to attract incomers both from the neighbouring countryside and from elsewhere.

Despite the growth in numbers which probably made it second only to Edinburgh among the Scottish burghs, the town's geographic extent was still very small because of the physical restrictions mentioned above. About three quarters of a mile long and hugging the shore line closely there is little doubt that the inhabitants of Dundee made full use of all the advantages of the site of their settlement from an early date. In this they were greatly helped by the award of burgh status at an early point in their history.

CHAPTER 2

Dundee, the Burgh

Dundee's Charter

When Earl David referred to 'my burgh' we may assume that by that time the king had given him a charter conferring burgh status on the settlement with Earl David as its feudal superior. William the Lion's charter in 1190 or 1191 may have been a favour to his brother but its consequences for Dundee were deeper and longer lasting.

Burghs with royal charters, later called Royal Burghs, were endowed with particular privileges until 1846, and retained a strong belief in their own vital place in the Scottish scheme of things even after that. This was expressed through the Convention of Royal Burghs until 1975, when local government reforms wiped away local councils and officials, the last practical remnants of the burghs' former constitutional and economic importance.

William's charter, if it ever existed as a written document as opposed to a verbal agreement with Earl David, had disappeared by the early fourteenth century. So important did Dundonians consider proof of their burghal status that they asked Robert I to confirm it. He did so in 1327 and his charter stated that all the evidence given both by local men and by burgesses from other places showed that Dundee had exercised burgh rights and privileges from the twelfth century. Later monarchs confirmed and extended these, most fully Charles I's great charter of 1641.

Management of the Burgh

Burgh status brought responsibilities as well as privileges, political and economic, which evolved through the centuries. By the fourteenth century the town seems to have had its own local government, in which perhaps all the burgesses shared, but by the sixteenth century when the population was much larger, the town was managed by a council consisting of a provost, four bailies or magistrates, several other burgesses and representatives of the Guildry and the incorporated trades, all elected, though not by what we would now term democratic means. Most councillors were

Part of the Charter granted by Robert the Bruce in 1327. The oldest existing charter giving burgh status, this is kept in Dundee City Archives. It has lost its seal but written in Latin on parchment it confirms the trading privileges belonging to Dundee from the time of William the Lion which boosted its prosperity throughout medieval and early modern times. *Dundee Archive and Record Centre.*

from the merchant class and by the sixteenth century from a very small section of even that select group.

In effect, Dundee like most other Scottish burghs was governed by a small, oligarchic clique. The retiring council had most say in the election of the new and also at times tried to exert pressure on the trades to appoint representatives from their membership who would suit the majority in the council.

The elections of the presiding provost and bailies became somewhat complicated as the old and new councillors got together and made out leets—short lists—of candidates for the positions of provost and bailies. These had to be sent to the Guildry and incorporated trades for them to vote on. Their returns were then sent back to the council for final election so that the process took a couple of weeks.

In 1360 effective financial independence was obtained by means of a feu-ferme charter granted by the burgh superior who by this time was the king. This allowed the burgh to handle all the revenue from its own taxes and property, known as the common good, in return for a fixed sum due to the superior, though of course national taxes like the great customs on exports were still paid to the crown.

It is perhaps easy to understand how power in the burghs became concentrated in so few hands, when one considers the responsibility that lay on magistrates and councillors in both local and national affairs. Royal Burghs were the third estate of the realm, after the clergy and the nobility, and expected to send representatives from their council to national meetings of these Three Estates, the Scottish Parliament. This was expensive not only for the burgh as the accounts of the Thesaurers (Treasurers) show, but also for those councillors whose attendance at parliament meant absence from their own business.

A representative from the Town Council was also sent to meetings of the Convention of Royal Burghs, which met annually from 1578—more expense for the town and delegate. The Convention had considerable influence over its members and membership brought obligations beyond simply attending meetings. Help had to be given to other burghs in time of trouble, when for example harbours were damaged by storms or vital bridges fell down, and when the annual meeting took place within a burgh the accounts show just how much that cost. Dundee was often the venue.

The Convention fined burghs for non-attendance unless express permission for absence had been given. In 1592 Dundee had to pay a fine of £20 Scots because no delegate was sent and in 1619 a fine of £19 Scots was imposed because the Dundonians left before the proceedings of the Convention ended. The Town Council also incurred communal expense when it appointed an agent to look after its affairs in Edinburgh. In 1613 Sir John Winram was paid £700 Scots for his services there.

The Burghs and the Law

A Royal Burgh also had its own court of law which magistrates had to administer. Within the burgh bounds, Dundee's own courts ruled on most questions of law and order, as well as on the burgh's own trade and building regulations. The magistrates were usually the senior councillors the Provost and Bailies.

Disputes between citizens involving property, physical assault and financial arrangements came before the burgh courts. Offenders could be fined, imprisoned, or put in the stocks. The ultimate and very potent punishment was banishment from the town; an expelled burgess could then no longer exercise his trade, nor could a licensed pauper legitimately beg. The threat of banishment, which looks like exporting one's own dirty linen, could bring all but the most recalcitrant to heel. Until the Reformation attempts to recover debts were dealt with by church courts.

Burgh councils and courts everywhere in Scotland were very careful of their reputation and authority. In June 1642 we find two Dundee burgesses being censured for pursuing witnesses before the sheriff instead of the burgh court, contrary to the acts of the burgh. In July 1615 John Gray was found guilty of striking the town's officer and pulling him to the ground. This was by implication an insult to the town's authority and Gray was punished by being confined in the tolbooth because he could not pay the fine; he was also compelled to go to where the offence took place and humbly beg pardon on his knees. On another occasion David Spankey was fined 10s Scots to be paid to the almshouse because he claimed there was 'no justice done in the tolbooth'.

The burgh Head Court met twice a year and then all the councillors were called to assist the magistrates' deliberations. Another time-consuming duty for the bailies was attendance at weekly markets. There they had to ensure that all the burgh's regulations were obeyed and taxes paid; for example that a ladle of grain or flour was taken for the town from each load. In 1592 the Convention of Royal Burghs tried without success to stop this practice which traders from outside Dundee resented. In 1633 it was found necessary to impose an unlaw, a fine, of £5 Scots if the bailies were absent from the market, as it had been discovered that they were not attending regularly.

Only the wealthy could easily afford office and the knowledge that fines were imposed on those who failed to attend once they were elected was certainly not an inducement to participate. Of course there were also 'perks' for magistrates, such as a creel of coal out of every cargo from Fife. They could also escape paying some taxes and received a share of some fines.

Burghal Responsibilities

Royal Burghs were also responsible for collecting any extraordinary taxes imposed by the monarch. Dundee had to assist with the costs of the wedding of Princess Elizabeth, daughter of James VI, to Frederick of the Palatinate in 1615. In 1636 4,000 merks were needed for the town's 'most necessarie debts specially their pairt of H M great taxation'. During the 1630s and 1640s Charles I's policies imposed a further burden. Indeed in 1642, the Town Council considered taking legal action against the magistrates because they had not paid their instalments of 'extraordar taxation'.

Despite the apparent handicaps that burgh status brought, few refused it as there were also undoubted corporate (and private) advantages, notably the monopoly—at least theoretically—of foreign trade and control over markets in the burgh's 'liberties'. In Dundee's case these liberties included Coupar Angus, Kirriemuir, Alyth and Kettins. Dundee's preeminent position brought it ever-increasing authority and importance from an early date.

By the end of the fourteenth century it was sending representatives to parliament, and in 1359 it had become a sheriffdom which must have induced much civic pride both for the honour itself and the income which this enhanced role generated. The sheriffdom however created much friction with the neighbouring sheriffdom of Forfar and seems to have been allowed to lapse.

The legal status of the burgh continued to be a matter of concern. In the sixteenth century the burgh authorities objected to cases being taken to other courts, especially those of the sheriff of the shire and Charles I was persuaded to grant a new gift of sheriffship to the town.

The sheriffdom did not remove all sources of annoyance, however, and could cause extra trouble for the burgh. One very expensive duty was the escorting of state prisoners between different areas of jurisdiction. Dundee on occasion had to pay for armed guards for such a prisoner, and their transport across the Tay to a Fife port or to Cupar to the Fife sheriff; on occasion they had to take the prisoner even further.

The Community of the Burgh

Two institutions found only in burghs were the Merchant Guild and the Incorporated Trades, both of which needed recognition from the burgh court in the shape of a Seal of Cause, authorising formal association. Dundee's Guild is believed to be one of the earliest founded in Scotland though the only existing Seal of Cause giving the merchants the power to elect a deacon is dated 1515. From the time of William I the Merchant Guild had been given the monopoly of buying and selling within the liberties of a burgh. This brought wealth and influence to the merchant class which helped them gain so much influence in burgh government.

The craftsmen were later in forming their associations throughout Scotland. In 1469 the Scottish Parliament gave them a share in electing burgh officers. The earliest Seal of Cause existing in Dundee is the Weavers', dated 1512. Other trades may have been granted formal status before but do not possess any records. Nine of these incorporations making and selling what would today be called 'consumer goods', the Baker Trade being the oldest, had formed a loose association by the middle of the sixteenth century and three building trades, Wrights,

Dundee's seal, showing St Clement on one side and St Mary on the other. The fact that both saints were depicted on the seal shows that both at one time were important to the burgh.

Masons and Slaters, which became incorporated in the seventeenth century, formed the United Trades in the eighteenth.

Parallel to the merchants' monopoly of buying and selling within the burgh were the privileges accorded to members of the craft incorporations, who alone had the legal right to practise their skills and train apprentices there. These incorporations also looked after their own members in sickness and old age, keeping their funds in their box or kist. The seamen were also allowed to form their own fraternity and in 1664, all merchants bringing goods into the harbour had to pay their primage, i.e. a gratuity in addition to freight charges, into the sailors' box. Maltmen too formed an independent association.

Not every merchant or craftsman automatically became a member of these associations. Only freemen were eligible and while everyone living within the official boundaries of the town had to obey the laws laid down by the Council and Head Court, not everyone became a freeman burgess. Freeman had to pay for the privilege and most Dundonians were only 'indwellers' who had no special privileges; on the other hand, they did not have to pay any of the 'great taxes' nor share in 'watch and ward', i.e. patrolling the burgh to keep the peace. These privileges and duties remained monopolies in theory at least until 1846. In the twentieth century being appointed a freeman of a burgh is merely a compliment to persons the burgh wishes to honour.

Prospectus Civitatis TAODUNI ab Oriente. (The Prospect of y Town of DUNDEE from y East.

Prospect of Dundee from the east, from Slezer's *Theatrum Scotiae*, late seventeenth century. One of the earliest sketches of Dundee known to exist. Taken from near Peep o' Day, this illustrates the harbour at the time, and demonstrates that Monck's order to destroy the walls had not been fully obeyed.

As well as respectable 'indwellers' there were also the poor, a group about whom few written records survive; mainly we read of them receiving charity, from the church funds, from private charities—and surprisingly—being kept out of the main parish church of St. Mary's, by the bellman during the week and by sergeants on holy days and Sundays!

The Constable

Burghs were of course subject to national law like every person and institution in Scotland but there was another legal restriction on Dundee's independence, the position of Constable. The Scrymgeour family held this hereditary office for centuries after William Wallace gave the post of Constable of Dundee castle to Alexander Scrymgeour in 1298. The post was made hereditary in the family in 1317.

The Constable could thereafter hold his barony court on the Castle Hill, and considering the burgh magistrates' self-conscious pride in their jurisdiction it is hardly surprising that over the centuries there was resistance to this crown official's authority. The scope for conflict was finally resolved only in 1747 when all heritable jurisdictions were finally abolished in the wake of the Forty-Five rebellion. In the centuries between, however, various adjustments were made to the relationship of town and Constable, loss to the latter often being compensated for by cash payments such as £1,800 in 1747.

From 1384 the Constable's legal rights in the burgh could be exercised only during the annual fair and even then the bailies went round the fair with him and imposed the fines. But there was often tension even though sometimes the leader of the Council, the Provost and the Constable were one and the same.

CHAPTER 3

The Economic Growth of the Burgh

Early Trade and Traders

It seems likely that Dundee was already a thriving commercial port when William the Lion gave the burgh its charter, but it could only benefit from the privileges that Earl David had won for it. Its merchants were managing to attract trade from St Andrews and Montrose as well as causing alarm in Perth whose burgesses obtained another charter from King William in an attempt to prevent further erosion of their previous monopoly over the Tay estuary and river by their upstart rival in the east. However, this had little effect and Dundee's trade continued to grow. Nevertheless it was 1602 before Perth finally accepted that the two burghs must share the trade that came to the Tay and the resulting responsibility towards managing sea lanes, customs, lights, etc.

There is clear proof that by the thirteenth century traders were coming to the burgh from all over Europe. As early as 1297 merchants from Lubeck did business with Dundonians. We know this because they were in trouble for leaving without paying their customs bill of £80 Scots—a considerable amount. Some years later, during the wars with England, Germans were arrested in Boston, Lincolnshire, for persisting with their Dundee trade.

What was bought and sold in the port? Early exports included hides and wool, much from Coupar Angus abbey for instance, the best in Scotland, in return for imports of wine and grain. The Flanders clothmakers used Scottish wool as well as English from the middle of the eleventh century. Grain was exported too, especially in years of good harvests, although this was not allowed in time of dearth.

The local fishing industry also brought in some revenue, though Dundee exports of salmon were only the sixth highest in the country, one year paying customs dues of a mere £14 Scots out of a total for Scotland of £310. In the early fourteenth century, raw wool and hides were the main export. In 1326–7 18 ships sailing from Dundee paid £240.4s.8d Scots customs duty for cargoes which included 68 lasts three sacks and nine stones of wool and 4,203 woolfells (sheepskins) as well as over seven lasts of hides. A last varied in weight but was roughly 4,000 lbs. Grey cloth and coloured 'material' were imported as well as dyed stuff for the king, and confections and pepper for the royal household. In 1264 wine was imported for the castles in Forfarshire.

An Early Textile Town

When the export of raw wool experienced recession in the fifteenth century, the townspeople and possibly also outworkers in the hinterland turned to using themselves the excellent and plentiful supplies from Coupar Angus; they made a coarse wool cloth and plaids and knitted bonnets which became Dundee specialities. In Bonnetmakers Row, now the Hilltown, for centuries men could be seen sitting outside their houses turning out their famous wares.

Once cloth making was established, the introduction of finishing processes tended to follow. The craft of the Litsters, the dyers, was soon established but dye had to be imported, some of it through Aberdeen; in 1498, James Guild of Dundee paid £20 Scots for woad bought in the northern town. At the end of the sixteenth century the town's imports of dyestuffs amounted to more than that of all the other Scottish burghs.

Despite this preeminence the Dundee litsters could not apparently cope with some processes, for David Wedderburn, the Dundee merchant whose *Compt Buik* tells us so much about business practices in Dundee between 1587 and 1630, records sending a tailor, Alexander Brown, to London with blue cloth which was to be dyed violet there.

Just how important cloth making was to Dundee must be a matter for conjecture. The export figures show that there was some volatility in markets. In the middle of the fifteenth century (1434/35) for example, only £6.19s.8d Scots was paid in customs duty on exports, only about 2% of the whole for Scotland. Hector Boece thought Dundee could be fairly described as a town where 'many and virtous and labouring pepill are in the makying of claith', but Bishop Leslie (c 1527–96) was uncertain whether Dundonians were richer from trading in 'outlandis geir and merchandise' i.e. foreign goods and trading, or from the results of their own labour and craftsmanship.

However, in the early seventeenth century, cloth and plaiding accounted for nearly 40% of all the manufactured goods that were exported from Scotland and a substantial proportion of that came from Dundee.

Home-grown wool was used and by the sixteenth century linen thread and cloth were also being spun and woven from home-grown and imported flax. But coarse woollen cloth, hides, skins and fish were for long the most important Dundee products to go overseas.

Gunmaking

One activity in which Dundee undoubtedly excelled was that of gunmaking. At the end of the sixteenth century Dundee was probably the foremost centre of the craft in Scotland. All master metalworkers were members of the Hammermen Trade whose Lockit Book containing the secrets of the trade was begun in 1587, when eight of the 35 master craftsmen were gunmakers.

Iron and brass were imported from the Low Countries and Sweden and there was a thriving export trade of Dundee guns to the Baltic countries, Germany and France; David Wedderburn sent 18 pistols to Spain in 1608.

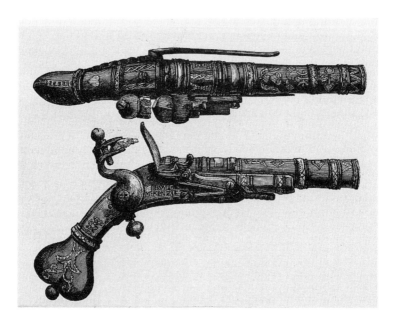

David McKenzie's was the last gunsmith in Dundee. Though Dundee's pre-eminence in gunmaking declined in the seventeenth century, there were still a few craftsmen in the burgh in the eighteenth (1712) who could produce beautiful weapons, as this example shows.

Scottish mercenaries leaving for service abroad in foreign armies would buy their weapons when passing through the town.

It is not certain whether the Dundee smiths made any type of pistol other than the fishtail and lemon butt but they were highly prized, perhaps more as a badge of rank than as a weapon. However, the trade decayed during the seventeenth century and by 1663 there were only two gunmakers among the Hammermen.

Dundee Trade in Early Modern Times

Textiles and guns were not the only sources of the town's prosperity. The safety of the harbour and the convenience of a town so centrally placed in Scotland had led to such increase in trade that by the second half of the sixteenth century, Dundee had become an entrepot port.

Grain, hides, fish, Orkney butter were among the raw materials collected there and shipped in and out along the Scottish coasts as far as Shetland, the outer Hebrides and abroad. Highland horses could regularly be bought in the burgh, both broken in and untamed. Coal came from the Forth coastal towns, timber, iron, pitch, tar, hemp, flax, wax, copper kettles from the Baltic, where 20 to 30 Dundee ships traded regularly. Luxury goods like spices, Bay salt (which had different qualities from home-made), exotic fruits and vegetables such as dates and onions and probably by the seventeenth century, oranges and lemons, made up parts of cargoes from Flanders, France and Spain. English goods also reached the port.

In 1535, Dundee was Scotland's second highest valued burgh, being assessed for the king's taxes at £321 compared to Edinburgh's £833, with Aberdeen close behind at £315 and next Glasgow trailing at £67, all Scots money of course. Edinburgh had by far the largest export trade in Scotland by the end of the sixteenth century, particularly in luxury goods, but Dundee's share was not to be sneered at, and Edinburgh merchants were inclined to leave the Scandinavian timber trade to the smaller port.

Trading Regulations

As trade was so important it is not surprising to find strict regulations being made to ensure fairness and reliability. Attempts were frequently made within the burgh, within the county of Forfar and nationally to

These Bakers' Weights, shaped like loaves, belonged to the Guildry and were used to ensure that bakers were making bread of the correct weight. One is the quartern (4lbs) weight and the other the half quartern (2 lbs). *Dundee Art Galleries and Museums.*

control weights and prices. The price and weights of food were set down by the Town Council and fines imposed for overcharging.

The bakers sometimes thought they were hardly done by and complained bitterly about the relative prices and weights set for loaves. In 1598 bakers and brewers too stopped work for a time in protest but eventually agreed to the prices fixed for grain by the Provost and bailies.

But there were difficulties about weights for many centuries. In 1555 the Scottish Parliament decreed that the same measure should be used for buying and selling, but in Dundee this was honoured more in the breach than in the observance. It was 1611 before the Town Council actually forbade the use of non-standard weights.

One Dundee practice caused great annoyance among traders coming to buy and sell in the burgh. Dundee weights were for long rather less than those of outsiders but Dundonians bought using the sellers' weights and sold using their own. Some local measures were taken to avoid discord between buyers and sellers. For instance one Dundonian, Alexander

Lawson, younger, was fined when he bought bear (barley) from an Englishman and made the weigher use different measures, four pecks in the boll difference.

In the tolbooth in the early seventeenth century a cooper was ordered to saw about half a foot off an oversized measure but the landward men were still suspicious and complained in 1643 that the burgh's measure was more than was allowed. The Council having asked some of their own number to try the measure accepted their decision that there was no difference and then fined the complainers!.

As well as the town's close watch on traders to maintain fair trading, individuals too guarded their reputation. Violet Rind accused of weighing wool 'with her elbocks', that is leaning her elbows on the scales, was incensed at the slander and took her accuser, Alex Henry, to court. There she was cleared and he was fined and further, had to beg her pardon.

The official weights were kept in the weighhouse. In 1590 lead was replaced by iron and new weights had to be supplied from Flanders. One of the conditions of the Union of 1707 was that weights and measures should be uniform in Scotland and England and in September 1708 the Dean of Guild reported to the council that he had received the British standard of weights and measures. A proclamation had to be made round the town that all burgesses and inhabitants were to bring their weights into line and to use no others after 1 November. This was a vain hope and it was many years before standard weights and measures were used throughout the United Kingdom.

Despite the many advantages of Dundee's situation one vital commodity always had to be imported into the burgh. This was fuel, as there was no peat nearby nor enough timber to provide wood for fires for the busy town. A strict watch was kept on the price of coal most of which came by sea from the Forth coal mines. Anyone who charged more than a merk (13s.4d Scots), a creel was fined four merks per chalder (c 96 imperial bushels).

The Mint and Money Matters

The reliability of coins was a matter of major concern when the amount of bullion they contained was more important than the face value which is what matters today. In 1567 Robert Jack, a merchant-burgess of Dundee, was hanged and quartered in Edinburgh for importing false money from Flanders.

The Dundee pint measure is one of the oldest standard measures in Scotland, having survived from the fifteenth or sixteenth century. The Scots was four times larger than the imperial pint. It could be divided into four mutchins or two chopins. *Dundee Art Galleries and Museums.*

There was regularly a shortage of bullion in Scotland which led to coins of all countries being accepted at recognised values. Small coins were in particularly short supply. Scottish mints were set up in various towns including Dundee until the end of the sixteenth century when Edinburgh became the main centre of coin production in Scotland.

There was a Dundee mint in Robert II's reign in the late fourteenth century when silver groats, half-groats, pennies and halfpennies were turned out though the output was always less than that of Perth and Edinburgh. In 1585 there was an outbreak of plague in Edinburgh which resulted in the temporary removal of the mint to Dundee but the disease soon reached the town and Perth was the mint's next destination.

The move to Dundee does not in any case seem to have been carried out very efficiently: the Privy Council received a report in December that no old 12 penny pieces, bawbees, placks and three penny groats were being brought in to the master cunyeor (coiner) to convert into new money. There is only one coin in existence, a half-plack, showing the distinguishing inner circle which both the Dundee and Perth mints were instructed to show on their coins. It is not known whether this was struck at Dundee or Perth but by 1588 the mint was back in Edinburgh.

After the Union of the Scottish and English Parliaments, a uniform coinage was established but there was still a shortage of small change and in the late eighteenth century in several towns tokens were issued by merchants and manufacturers. These tokens were meant to be worth their face value and were initially of good weight. They were of course illegal but they were tolerated as they filled a necessary gap. The most populous towns produced most of these but Dundee alone issued shillings as well as copper pennies, halfpennies and farthings.

Control of Trade and Traders

In Scotland generally great stress was laid on preventing monopolies and profiteering. Forestalling and regrating were forbidden by most burghs. Forestalling was the practice of buying goods before they reached the open market thereby avoiding tolls, and regrating was the practice of buying up and hoarding large quantities to sell later at a profit.

Because bread was such an important part of everyone's diet the Dundee magistrates in times of shortage restricted the amount of grain any one person could buy to what was needed in his own household. An Edinburgh merchant, James Ker, defied the magistrates by buying corn in bulk in July 1611 and though incarcerated in the tolbooth, returned in August and repeated his offence. When he was ordered to buy only enough for his own household for eight days, he declared that he cared nothing for the bailies of Dundee and would buy 'as meikle victual as he pleased'. And he would not bow his head to the bailie. He ended up in prison again and was fined £10 Scots in addition, but when he complained to the Court of Session he was ordered back to Dundee to go into ward in the tolbooth—at his own expense—until he had apologised to the magistrates for troubling them.

As well as controls on weights, prices and quantities, another restriction was placed on trading in most Royal Burghs. Control was exercised over home and foreign markets to ensure that the local guild merchants had the monopoly of buying and selling within the burgh bounds and its

The Weighhouse, built in St Clement's kirkyard in 1561 by George Lovell, Dean of Guild, who was sold part of the kirkyard on condition that he provided this building. It stood in one of the roads to the harbour until Crichton Street was built.

liberties. 'Stranger' merchants could not walk in and freely buy or sell goods; they had to pay various dues from which the guildry members were exempted. Another advantage the local merchants possessed was that any ship bringing a cargo into the port had to offer the local guild merchants the first chance to buy.

When the manufacturing of goods began to develop, attention was paid by the magistrates to the quality and quantity of what was being marketed. Of course these regulations were not always faithfully kept. In 1667 David Wemyss, a Dundee merchant, took action against his fellow townsmen before the Scottish Privy Council to ensure that weavers paid him £20 Scots for every web of linen worked since Lammas 1666 which was less than the prescribed one ell and two inches broad.

Fairs

One early proof of the importance of Dundee as a market town was the fact that a fair was established there in the thirteenth century. In many other burghs, even Edinburgh, there is often no definite evidence for such an event. The first known fair was held on 23 November, the date of the martyrdom of St Clement, the patron saint of the town until the twelfth century, when devotion to St Mary resulted in the church 'in the fields' being built in her honour and Our Lady's taking St Clement's place. (Both can be seen in the town's coat of arms.)

The Lady Mary Fair took place on 15 August. The Scrymgeours established yet another on the day of the Nativity of the Virgin, originally 8 September then 19 September. In the early eighteenth century Stobs Fair began, on Stobsmuir. Fairs were days of considerable excitement for the local people. Exotic goods would be on show while the usual restrictions on trading were removed. Only those who broke the 'peace of the fair' were arrested.

Early Problems

By 1350 Dundee was recognised as one of the four great burghs in the country, ranking below Edinburgh but being considered almost equal with Aberdeen and Perth. The burgh's rise to prosperity was not smooth, however, as the taxation lists show. With much of its trade being dependent on exports, minor as well as major events elsewhere could have a disproportionate effect. For instance, troubles in the Baltic affected the cloth trade as well as that in skins and hides in the sixteenth century.

Then there was always the risk of piracy, endemic in European waters, although some Dundonians practised piracy as well as suffering from it. In 1668, John Ramsay of Dundee and some other seamen from Perth, Elie, Woodhaven and South Ferry were suspected of that crime and were sent to Leith to be re-examined after questioning in Dundee.

The burgesses did their best to counter adverse trading conditions, changing from one type of goods and craft to another but often they had little control over events. They could do little to avert the tragedy that hit Scotland at the end of the thirteenth century. King Alexander III (1241–86) died in a storm on the south shores of Fife and his heiress, his granddaughter, the Maid of Norway, never set foot on Scottish soil. On her way to Scotland, she died on the Orkney islands which were then Danish.

Edward I of England thought he could seize the opportunity to take over the northern country but his overt ambition roused resistance. It is said that Dundee was the scene of a fight which sparked off William

Wallace's stand against Edward. He is reputed to have attended school in the town and after he killed the Dundee governor's son in a squabble, he was outlawed. He became leader of some of the Scots who wanted to be rid of Edward and the English. In the succeeding Wars of Independence, Dundee changed hands several times. Whenever war between Scotland and England broke out, or during civil strife, the town tended to be besieged and ransacked. The Tay was an obvious road to the heart of the country and Dundee was in the way of any naval force attempting to use the waterway, while land forces were bound to try to keep control of the town to prevent the use of the Tay by invaders. Clearly this disadvantaged its trade but the burgh seemed to have a notable capacity for recovery.

During the 'Rough Wooing' in the 1540s when Henry VIII tried to win Mary, Queen of Scots, as wife for his son, later Edward VI, the town suffered badly and during the following wars over religion Dundee was attacked by the English and by Scots with French support. Almost forty years after the turmoil, in 1582, the Privy Council allowed the town some relief from taxes in response to a petition that so many houses had been 'brunt and cassit doon by the English'.

Its tax assessment dropped slightly in the 1580s and 1590s showing that the claim of shortage of money was not without justification. Despite this however, there is evidence at the same period from the fairly extensive building that went on, public and private, that the town was not unprosperous. The recovery was to be relatively short-lived, however, and as will be seen later, the seventeenth century saw the most devastating effects of national and international strife.

CHAPTER 4

Social Life

The Trappings of Domestic Life

How did people live in the burgh in medieval and early modern times?
What did they eat? How did they spend any leisure time? How did they
earn their living? For the earliest times, little evidence now survives. What
we can say though is that people were much less trammelled with
possessions, both domestic and personal, than most of us are today.

Housework was clearly less demanding when furniture consisted simply
of a table and benches or stools, a kist for storage of the few household
goods, beds, probably box-beds, their wooden base softened only by straw
in most houses, although the wealthier aspired in later centuries to feather
beds and even sheets. Straw or rushes also were mostly used for floor
coverings, if the bare earth at ground floor level or the wooden boards
upstairs were covered at all. This material collected all the dirt that fell from
dirty feet and from cooking and eating, and cleaning was done by throwing
it out at intervals. There were few separate apartments and privacy was a
scarce commodity, probably not missed, even among the wealthy.

Hygiene

Standards of hygiene were very different then. With every drop of water
having to be collected from the various wells in the town or from the burns,
there was little incentive for obsessive cleanliness either of clothing or of
person. Indeed, wells could be a source of entertainment for women who
enjoyed a good gossip in the queue while waiting their turn.

Today we complain of the smell of petrol or diesel fumes. In medieval
Dundee it is probable we would not find any more acceptable the smell
of rarely washed people and clothes, of horse dung and street middens of
household and business waste from the various trades and shops.

Not that street cleanliness was neglected in the town, and from very
early times there was concern for the environment. Though middens in

Four eighteenth century wells in use until 1860 and closed up after the Lintrathen water scheme was in use.

the street were a necessary part of life, attempts were made to mitigate the nuisance. In 1559 the Town Council ordered that middens were to be removed from the streets on pain of a fine of 8s Scots or imprisonment in the Steeple. A few years later restrictions were placed on where dirt could be dumped. Rubbish was to be put in the sea and anyone who emptied a household closet too near the town would be found in the stocks.

In 1591 the new hangman, Michael Mores, became also the first public street cleaner. He was provided with a wheelbarrow and paid 2s.8d Scots per week and was expected to clean the area between Burial Wynd and Burnhead every 24 hours, elsewhere every two days.

The Council's actions do not seem to have been very successful for in the 1660s filthy streets were still a problem. At that time it was decided that each quarter of the town was to be patrolled by four or five constables and fines were to be laid on all who kept middens at their doors longer than twenty-four hours. It was even necessary in 1665 to send the town drummer round the town to announce that there would be a fine of £5 Scots on all who emptied their filth and closets into the kirkyard or the streets. And instead of throwing their household rubbish into the sea, some irresponsible characters were merely 'ca'ing their muck' out at the West port, where no doubt it would provide a noisome welcome to visitors to the town.

Infectious Diseases

Lack of knowledge of how diseases spread and of elementary hygiene resulted in epidemics of infections such as plague, bubonic and pneumonic, carried by fleas from rats. It is believed now that sometimes typhus was confused with plague but the effects were similar. From 1349 there were outbreaks in Scotland of what the Scots had gleefully called before that date 'the foul death of the English'.

Drastic steps were taken to keep it out of the burgh during an epidemic and to control it once it arrived. The harbour could be closed to ships from infected ports and the Fife ferry service restricted or stopped altogether, as in 1645, when the burgh suffered its last visitation. The 'Sick men's Yaird' was provided beyond Blackscroft to isolate those infected.

When the disease took two years to run its course in 1607 and 1608, it caused social and economic chaos. Life in the burgh became so disorganised that there were no elections to the Town Council and some councillors fled the town, returning only when threatened in 1608 with being 'put to the horn'. (This is a Scottish legal process outlawing those concerned.) An extra £1,000 Scots was required in taxes to pay the extra expenses involved in separating the sick from the healthy, in disinfecting or destroying goods belonging to those affected and in paying for the soldiers needed both to keep order generally and to protect the special cleaners carrying out these duties. Not only the poor and needy resented seeing their small stock of possessions damaged by being disinfected in kiln or kettle.

The schoolmaster lost fees, and the miller who was the tenant of the town's mills lost so much custom he demanded abatement of rent. Even the town knock (clock) stopped because the knock-keeper, Patrick Ramsay, had fled and had to be tempted back with double pay of £40 Scots.

Leprosy was the other disease most feared in medieval times. Sufferers were almost permanently isolated in leper houses outside burgh boundaries. Dundee's was near the Dens burn and lepers could come into town only to buy necessities on a few specified occasions.

There were other diseases related to poor hygienic conditions and infestations of worms, lice and fleas were commonplace. All infectious complaints such as smallpox, tuberculosis and no doubt the common cold spread quickly in the congested living conditions.

Cooking and Eating

What these earlier Dundonians ate and cooked came mainly from the surrounding area. Meal was ground from the crops produced in the crofts just outside the burgh and its hinterland and from Fife. They included oats, wheat, rye and bear, the last used largely for making ale which was the principal drink of all Scots until the price of tea and coffee dropped to what all could afford. Sometimes after a poor harvest and resulting dearth, grain had to be imported from abroad.

Some vegetables and fruit were grown in the gardens inside the burgh boundaries and wild fruits, herbs and plants would also be picked seasonally to supplement the diet. Fish was caught in the Tay and beef was the main meat eaten, though mutton, venison, goat meat and pork from the pigs that could be seen foraging round the streets, also appeared on Dundee plates. Hens would be seen in many gardens and wild fowls were also brought to the table.

In the earliest times, a fire on the floor in the middle of the house with the smoke going out through a hole in the roof would provide heat and cooking facilities. Later fireplaces with chimneys in the walls were used and sometimes even ovens in the homes of the wealthier. Light came from simple oil lamps and candles as well as the fire. Cutlery and kitchen utensils, mostly of pewter or wood, were few, but a knife was part of everyone's accoutrements though forks were not considered essential. Spoons were needed for supping broth and stirring the food in iron cooking pots.

Social Class

Society in the town was mixed and because of the compact nature of the medieval burgh all ranks rubbed shoulders in the streets. The beggar, the skilled craftsman, the wealthy merchant, the priest and the noble lived cheek by jowl in Dundee for many centuries, but they were not equal. Externally they were distinguished by the quality of their clothing— coarse cloth of various types for the majority, finer linen, imported silk and velvet for the wealthy—and perhaps only rags for the very poorest. Members of some trades could be identified by their dress, like the mason with his apron, and while servants were normally very plainly dressed, they could sometimes be very grand in their employers' cast-offs.

Clothes generally were of long-lasting material and in days when fashions did not change rapidly it was considered no shame to wear garments inherited from one's parents. Snobbery however was much in evidence. The merchants did not like their wives going around in aprons like the lower classes and members of crafts who looked dirty because of the materials they used were not welcome as guild brethren.

It is most difficult to ascertain the conditions of the poorer groups in society. They left no written wills and testaments, no letters, no bills paid or unpaid. One thing we can be sure of is that few lived so long as the average modern Dundonian. In the twentieth century it is increasingly realised that poverty reduces resistance to disease, whatever the advantages of modern medical knowledge and practice: in medieval Dundee it is unlikely that many of the poor could afford the skills of contemporary physicians, however primitive these may have been. No doubt they had recourse to folk remedies but we may assume that their rate of mortality was higher than that of the upper ranks of society.

Those most likely to succumb to disease among the better-off would be the very young, the very old and women bearing or giving birth to children. But all classes and ages suffered death and maiming from the fire of the various armies that attacked the town.

Work in the Burgh

There were many ways of earning a living in the burgh. Fishermen were probably the first occupants. There were butchers, bakers and candlestick-makers, cow keepers to look after the animals on their way to pasture, horsehirers, innkeepers, blacksmiths, silver and goldsmiths, gunsmiths; masons, slaters and wrights who could be joiners, painters, glaziers or cabinet makers, who looked after the fabric of Dundee's buildings and provided its inhabitants with the necessary furniture. There were maids, not only in the wealthier establishments, priests, schoolmasters, chirurgeons (surgeons), midwives, knife-grinders, in fact every possible trade that was necessary for the maintenance of urban life.

Not all would make a good living or be able to save for their old age or for poverty caused by illness or infirmity. Poor relief could be obtained from the church poor fund, or for the luckier from their trade's stock or from some other private charity. For those without even that assistance, begging was the last resort for the honest; again for the lucky ones, licensed begging, officially recognised, while no doubt theft would also be a way of life for the less honest. At times, there was an almshouse or hospital where a few 'puir and sick' men were installed.

Entertainments

Life was hard but there were festive occasions too, when for example the popular pageants featuring the Abbot of Unreason, then later, Robin Hood and Little John, were performed in the streets. May plays such as these were never popular with the authorities because of the excitement they engendered and in fact they were forbidden in 1555 when Mary of Guise was Queen Regent. The ban however does not seem to have been totally effective.

More formal entertainment was to be had when the miracle plays were performed in the Playfield, a piece of ground just outside the western town boundaries. The town and sometimes the craft incorporations were responsible for these, and the long list of the 'play-gear' that belonged to the town show that there must have been large casts, for it includes 60 crowns and 23 heads of hair. Unfortunately the list is all that remains. The crafts in all the large Scottish towns were responsible for producing pageants in honour of their patron saints but the only one about which we know much in Dundee, because of the loss of records, is the procession of Saint Crispin, illustrated in a frieze in the museum.

John Wedderburn's plays were also performed in the Playfield in the 1550s, plays such as '*John the Baptist*', which pointed out abuses in the old church. As has been suggested, the Reformation did not immediately stop such amusements in Dundee. In 1595–6, the burgh was subsidising plays performed by the High School and in 1601 an English company of players reached the town.

The Procession of St Crispin. St Crispin was the patron saint of the cordiners, the shoemakers. The Trade commissioned Alexander Methven, a local amateur artist, to paint a frieze of the procession for their room in the Trade Hall. Eventually finished by Henry Harwood in 1822 when the last procession took place, the frieze was removed bodily to Dundee Museum when the Hall was about to be demolished in the nineteenth century improvements to the centre of the town. This section shows King Crispin, who may have become transformed into a king as opposed to a saint after the Reformation. *Dundee Art Galleries & Museums.*

As one of the largest Scottish burghs Dundee must have been visited throughout the ages by the travelling musicians, players and jesters who made a living by moving round the country amusing all who would watch them in return for money or food. They added colour and liveliness to burgh life and on the occasions when the royal court came to the town, the minstrels, tumblers and dancing girls who performed for the king and queen also provided sideshows for the burgesses.

CHAPTER 5

The Reformation

Changes in Religion

There were more profound and philosophical elements in medieval Dundee life, however. The present-day traveller approaching Dundee from the south cannot but be aware of the importance of religion and education in the town. Though high rise flats and floodlit football stadia are now the dominant man-made features on the skyline, church spires and schools are still prominent. In the middle of the sixteenth century and the early seventeenth the medieval burgh was to see drastic changes during the violence that arose in the melee of religious change and international diplomacy that divided Christianity in western Europe into Roman Catholics and Protestants. Dundee's prosperity as well as its appearance was to suffer during this period.

From a very early point in its existence the Christian church, that is the universal Catholic church, had been subject to attempts at purification and reform. Sometimes the would-be reformers were categorised as heretics, sometimes like the monastic orders, two of which had friaries in Dundee, they were absorbed into the mainstream of the Church.

Most disruptive however was the sixteenth century Reformation which resulted in the formation of a second major form of Christianity, Protestantism. Martin Luther's protest against abuses in the church in 1517 is usually cited as the beginning of the movement which soon gathered impetus in Europe. Dundee's long history of European connections made it almost inevitable that knowledge of the new doctrines would soon spread within the burgh. They found a sympathetic hearing in many quarters where the apparent wealth of the friaries, as well as some growing dislike of idolatry roused much wrath.

There was still great loyalty and attachment to the church and old ways, as can be seen from the continuing gifts to St Mary's until well on in the century, but what was important in Dundee was that quite early in the history of Protestantism, the reform movement gained support from the most influential members of society and from the Provost and Town Council.

Local Support for Reform

Signs of local sympathy for reforming doctrines, or at least for those who criticised them, appeared fairly early in the burgh. In the early 1530s the Council and townspeople gave shelter to Alexander Alane, or Alesius, and Friar Alexander Dick who had fled from other burghs, St Andrews and Aberdeen, to avoid punishment for their heretical views.

Among Dundonians the Wedderburn brothers, James, John and Robert, were foremost in expressing criticism of the abuses they could see in the church. Their father James had probably assisted Alesius in his eventual escape from Scotland. One of the brothers, James, a merchant like his father, also wrote plays using these as such potent vehicles for his satire on abuses in the church that he had to fly to France to escape arrest and later he died there. His tragedy of *John the Baptist* was performed in the Playfield. He also joined with his brother John in composing the *Gude and Godlie Ballads*.

John who had also had to fly the country returned in 1542 at a time when repression of heretics was not so active. About 1544 he had the ballads published in Dundee by John Scott, an early printer. Many of the poems and hymns in the collection had been circulating in the town and beyond before then and their witty expression of anti-papal and anti-Mass doctrines must have made the orthodox Roman Catholics feel that the devil certainly had the best tunes.

The Wedderburns were not the only inhabitants who suffered for their reforming sympathies during these years. One merchant, James Rollock, forfeited all his property when he fled to Campvere instead of appearing before an ecclesiastical tribunal to defend himself on the charge of heresy, but he was able to return in 1551. The most famous reformer connected with Dundee is George Wishart. Like other scholars he had spent time in England, Germany and Switzerland, returning in 1543 to his home at Pitarrow near Dundee when it seemed that pro-reform elements were in power.

When Cardinal Beaton gained the ascendancy in government, however, Wishart was not only forbidden to preach in Dundee, he was ordered to leave the town. Though he bowed to Beaton's mandate for some time, he returned on hearing of an outbreak of plague in the town. Such courage made him a hero there as well as a spiritual comforter. Beaton obviously recognised him as an opponent to be feared and unsuccessful attempts were made to assassinate him in Dundee and Forfarshire. Eventually Wishart was captured and put to death by burning just outside St Andrews

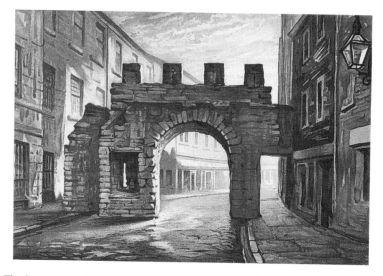

The Cowgate Port, known erroneously as the Wishart Arch, but probably built when the town's defences were being strengthened in the 1590s.

Castle on 1 March 1546. He had been extremely influential in the Scottish reform movement, both in his doctrines and in organising would-be reformers, particularly in Dundee.

Both France and England had been using the minority of Mary, Queen of Scots, to fight out their religious and diplomatic differences in Scotland and it has been suggested that Wishart was an English agent sent to try to assassinate Cardinal Beaton, but the verdict on this has to be 'Not Proven'. After his death some of his supporters captured St Andrews Castle, killed Beaton and withstood for some time a seige by French and Scottish forces. An English invasion culminating in their victory at Pinkie in 1547 came too late to save the besieged, including John Knox, and had dire effects on Dundee.

Dundee in Enemy Hands

In the English campaigns in 1547–48 and in the following years Broughty Castle was held by an English garrison, and the town itself was badly damaged. The steeple of St Mary's was fortified and used by the English forces to threaten the population. By the time they left, the interior of the church had been grievously looted, much of the building had been demolished and the bells in the steeple removed.

However, enthusiasm for religious reform survived even the material hardships of the occupation and the association of Protestantism with the 'Auld Enemy of England'. If we are to believe the commander at Broughty, most Dundonians disliked priests and had asked him for English translations of the Bible, which he said he had promised them.

It was 1551 before the English departed, only to be replaced by French forces supporting the Queen Mother, Mary of Guise. What was obviously French occupation became as distasteful to the Scots as English occupation had been, in Dundee as elsewhere. When Elizabeth became Queen of England and indicated her support for Protestantism, the rebel Lords of the Congregation, a group largely though not all in favour of religious reform, enrolled her assistance and in 1560, the French left and the church in Scotland began to be organised according to the reformed doctrines.

Changing Beliefs

During these years in Dundee as in the rest of Scotland change in religious beliefs did not overwhelm the whole population. It must be remembered that while support for reform existed, the old faith still attracted both spiritual loyalty and material gifts. What swayed the balance in Dundee was the reforming zeal of so many of the influential men in the town. The wealthy Wedderburns and Provost Scrymgeour were early examples. In 1553 James Haliburton became Provost and under him the town's adherence to Protestantism strengthened. Simply, he could not have been elected had there not been sympathy with his views on the Town Council which soon showed its Protestant colour.

When the master of the grammar school, Thomas MacGibbon, lost pupils because he was discussing the new doctrines in class, the Council insisted that their fees must be paid to MacGibbon even though they had gone to study under another master. When a prominent Dundee Protestant preacher, Paul Methven, a baker to trade, was threatened with arrest, it was Provost Haliburton who apparently warned him to fly the town. Haliburton was a skilful military leader in the fight against the troops of Mary of Guise and was also one of the signatories of the First Book of Discipline, which laid out the reformers' aims. He was to be Provost with only a short break until 1589.

Dundee Churches after the Reformation

The church of Dundee was to be very different both materially and spiritually after the Reformation. St Mary's church itself stood desolate for some years after the damage done by English forces in 1548. The Town Council appointed a councillor as Kirkmaster in 1562 to take charge of repair and maintenance of the church, but the renovation after 1560 had to cater for the very different type of church service and provided simple interiors in the several churches that replaced the lavishly decorated parish church that stood there before.

The choir, nave and transepts were transformed into three and then four separate churches. First, St Mary's, the East or later, the Old Kirk, was housed in the choir and chancel, then the Cross Church as a single congregation in the transept until 1582, when the south part became the South Church. The nave was used as a quarry until 1584 when yet another church was erected there. Pews were built in the churches for the first time and these were the property of individuals or institutions; the Trades for instance had their own pews and paid their own cleaners as well as doorkeepers to make sure that only members and their families used these seats. The poor were not really welcomed at services in the parish church even before 1560.

As far as the actual buildings are concerned the town kirks have had chequered careers. In 1645, in Montrose's attack on the town, the church nearest the Steeple was burned and from then until 1789, when the present Steeple Church was built, the Old Steeple stood separate from the town churches. Monck used the Cross church as a stable but the worst disaster that overtook them in modern times was the dreadful fire of 1841 which destroyed all but the Steeple church and, an irreparable loss, the valuable library of rare incunabula which had been housed in the East Church.

The Victory of the Reformers

The Scottish reformed church and therefore its congregations in Dundee did not immediately after 1560 become presbyterian. There was a long divisive struggle, usually involving the Scottish monarch, before the office of bishop was abolished in the Scottish Kirk. Dundee Protestants tended to sympathise with the anti-episcopalian line and in 1580 a meeting of the Assembly in Dundee explicitly condemned episcopacy. One kirk session was formed in the burgh for all the congregations of the town churches in Dundee, which was and is unusual. Some of its ministers, like

William Christison, were prominent in the Assembly and indeed Christison became Moderator in 1569.

Neither the Reformation nor Presbyterianism won outright victories in 1560. Priests of the old church retained their income and in Dundee we even find a friar, John Black, being maintained as long as he kept the town clock in order.

The Roman Catholic church mounted the Counter-Reformation and this must have struck a sympathetic chord in some Dundee hearts, for two Jesuits were to be found proselytising and being sheltered there in the early seventeenth century. However, by the middle of the eighteenth century there were reputedly only three papists in a population of about 12,500. Nor was respect for the church always so great as we are sometimes led to believe. In 1565, it was reported that bairns were playing in the kirkyard and breaking the windows of the parish kirk.

Education in the Burgh

Nevertheless, the church and churchmen had been dominant in so many areas of life, both secular and religious, that the Reformation was bound to have profound and wide-reaching effects. One of the major responsibilities of the church in medieval times was education and there is a long history of schools in Dundee. The Bishop of Brechin granted Lindores Abbey the right to found schools in the burgh, a right that Pope Gregory IX confirmed soon after 1239. Whether the monks actually began teaching in the town is not known, but schools there were and some demand for education in medieval times though it was 1434 before the Brechin Diocesan Register first mentions an existing Dundee school.

The church usually maintained grammar and 'sang' schools. The grammar school provided a classical education to train future priests who might also become state servants, like Cardinal Beaton. The sang school's main task was to train boys to take part in religious services in which music was very important. The Bishop kept strict control over everything in the schools, in 1435 even censuring a master, Lawrence Lownan, because he built a new schoolhouse without express permission.

The sixteenth century saw control moving into the hands of the burgh authorities even before the Reformation. Though both a grammar and a sang school were attached to St Mary's, when one was burned by the English in 1548 it was the Town Council which rented premises to replace it, possibly within the other church of St Clement's.

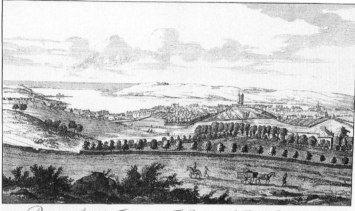

Prospectus Civitatis TAODUNI. The Prospect of ŷ Town of DUNDEE.

Prospect of Dundee from the north by Captain John Slezer in *Theatrum Scotiae*. Taken from between the Law and Dudhope Castle. The hospital is shown on the right of the picture marking the course of the Nethergate. The turreted building near the centre is the tolbooth, removed when the town house was built in the eighteenth century.

We have seen the influence the Town Council had as early as 1559 on the question of what Thomas Macgibbon taught. The Book of Discipline advocated education for all, town councils being the bodies responsible in the burghs. Most took this seriously and jealously protected their rights; teachers unauthorised by the Dundee council were on occasion imprisoned in the tolbooth.

One sign that the town was recovering at least some of its prosperity in the second half of the sixteenth century was that a new grammar school was built in 1588–89. The need for it had been recognised twenty years before but funds were not then available. The new school stood behind the new tolbooth in the Marketgait, and the town had used both hospital funds and shore silver to fund its construction as well as £100 Scots no longer needed for ordnance to defend against the Spanish Armada. The two-storey building housed the school until near the end of the eighteenth century when another was built in St Mary's churchyard. Thereafter the old one was used by the town guard and as a court room.

After the Reformation town councils took ever greater control of schools within their bounds. They were responsible for the schoolmasters' basic pay as well as the school building. In 1636 the Dundee councillors thought it would be a 'dangerous preparative' to augment the salary of Mr James Gleg, even though he had served with 'fidelity and care' for more that twenty years without any increase. However, they did give him a grant of £100 Scots for each of the four years during which his son, Thomas, attended St Andrews University.

It is interesting to find that a sang school was continued, now called the Music School, despite the decreasing share music took in religious services. The school had been reopened by 1584 with John Williamson as the first master.

In 1609 Mr John Mow or Maw was appointed to teach music as well as reading and writing; he had also to take the psalm in the East Kirk daily before evening and morning prayers. Apart from his salary of 200 merks he gave singing lessons for 13s.4d Scots quarterly, and instrumental lessons for 16s.8d Scots, while reading and writing brought him only 6s.8d Scots per pupil. Maw's fervent interest in music was to be further demonstrated when he became a burgess, for he chose to give a pair of virginals to the Town Council and the community. By 1647 his successor was able to charge 46s.8d Scots for music and writing, but burgesses' bairns paid only 30s Scots.

The Music School continued to prosper even after Monck's depredations. A gallery had been added in 1650 and a successful attempt was made to restore it only nine months after the sacking of the town. In 1677 the master, Alex Reid, requested heating for the 'very cold room' in which he taught where the temperature was doing his musical instruments no good at all. The Music School finally merged with other schools in the burgh in the eighteenth century when the Town council gave up insisting on its monopoly in teaching music.

Life after the Reformation

One admirable aim of the reformers was the achievement of an orderly, well-behaved society and accordingly, private morals came under closer scrutiny than had been usual in the past. The numbers of adulterers and fornicators seemed to increase sharply and indeed, Dundee needed a new prison especially for those who committed this 'horrid crime'. Very conveniently this was situated at the east end of the East Kirk, just above the meeting-place of the kirk session.

To modern eyes, one of the more horrific aspects of religious life in Europe from the late sixteenth to the early eighteenth centuries was the persecution of men and women—mostly women—believed to be witches. To judge from the written records, Dundee does not seem to have been very busy in this, though witches were certainly put to death there. There is a report that Regent Moray had 'a company of witches' burned on his visit to the town in 1569 and in November 1669 the Privy Council commissioned John Tarbet, the Provost, the Dean of Guild and several gentlemen of Angus to try Grissell Jaffray for the 'horrid cryme of witchcraft'. She was subsequently found guilty and sentenced to death.

There is one earlier proof of the town's involvement in this type of persecution. The Treasurer's accounts of 1590/91 give the detailed cost of having a witch put to death, the total coming to £5.16s.2d Scots. The cost of the rope, payment to the hangman, creelfulls of coal, 'twa tar barrels' and the carriage to the Playfield of everything needed are included. There the burning of the 'wiche', whose name is not given, would be a public spectacle, perhaps enjoyed somewhat gruesomely by at least some of the spectators as much as the plays and processions normally enacted there before strict Calvinism gained control.

Dundee and Dundonians were in the mainstream of religious life during these stirring changes in the sixteenth century. What happened in the town reflected national and international events. Both spiritual and economic life were affected, initially very disruptively, but by the end of the century the town had overcome the worst material effects and was as stable spiritually as could be expected during these turbulent years.

CHAPTER 6

Dundee in the Civil Wars

The Beginning of the Troubles

The town prospered in the late sixteenth and early seventeenth centuries, as its economy thrived. Unfortunately, like the rest of the British Isles, the town suffered from the Civil Wars caused by antagonism to Charles I's religious, economic and constitutional policies. Many of his subjects rebelled, the Scots being the first, starting the Bishops' Wars in 1639 shortly after the signing of the National Covenant in 1638.

The king had to make peace with the Scots, and hoping for support against the recalcitrant English parliament tried to make enough concessions to reconcile them. Charles's granting the so-called Great Charter to Dundee in 1641 was probably part of this policy. However the English parliamentary side was more successful with the Scots and the two were party to the agreement known as the Solemn League and Covenant in 1643. Scottish armies thereafter fought for a time for the parliamentary side in the Civil War. In November 1643, copies of the two Covenants were laid up in the town's charter kist.

Dundee and the Army

As the second wealthiest Scottish burgh, Dundee was deeply involved in raising men, supplies and funds. In 1643 and 1644 the Town Council was very busy. In March and April 1643 though declaring willingness to give money for the relief of the Scottish army in Ireland, they told the Earl of Argyll that they had none, while an appeal to the merchants in the town brought the same response. In December of that year, however, the town had to face a tax bill of £14,313.2s.2d Scots, their share of £92,000 Scots imposed by the government.

In addition the town had to raise a company and their agents had to find 15 or 16 baggage horses—none to cost more than 50 merks—as well as collecting cloth to take to the tailors to make 'sogers coats'. On 26

December 1643, the magistrates and members of the incorporations had to go round the town to round up everyone designated to join the company and they were told there was to be no interruption 'till the company be maid up'.

All the burgesses too had to be armed for a muster of the shire or be fined £20 Scots and lose their freedom. Ammunition and the magazine of powder were stored in the windmill near the new harbour. The Council however does not seem to have been desperately enthusiastic about making up a company. It tried to argue that 150 men with baggage carriers was a sufficient contribution from Dundee and sent on the bailies to Forfar, the county town, to demonstrate the burgh's inability to raise 200 men. The spiritual welfare of the populace was not neglected either, for the Council also tried to persuade the Presbytery not to send any of the town's ministers with the 1643 expedition.

Defence of the Burgh

The town itself had to be guarded. In October 1643 a night watch of 20 men was set up until it 'please the land to settle the present troubles', with ensigns in charge in each quarter of the town. Throughout 1644 and 1645 the burgh's defences were strengthened, houseowners with back dykes on the Overgate and Murraygate being instructed in April 1644 to repair them with stone and mortar to a good height or to incur a fine of £20 Scots.

In October the Council decided to finish work on the fortifications with voluntary contributions and in May 1645 ordered that houses outside the fortifications should be demolished, thereby removing possible shelter for any attackers. In the meantime, when the earl of Montrose, who by this time supported the king against the Scottish Estates, captured Perth, at least one Dundonian, Robert Lundy, fled to St Andrews. For this coward-ice he was censured and fined 300 merks in 1644.

All these preparations did not protect the burgesses from the onslaught that Montrose launched against the town. On 4 April 1645 he took the defenders completely by surprise and stormed into Dundee. It was per-haps fortunate that he was closely pursued by the army of the Covenant or the burgh might have suffered the sort of sack that Aberdeen had been subjected to. Montrose had to gather his forces together after only a few hours in the town and make his way north for safety.

Despite the short time his Highlanders and Irishmen were in Dundee, however, they had managed to inflict damage for which the town later received over £54,000 Scots compensation. Despite the effects of this raid, it is interesting to find that when Montrose was eventually defeated and captured and led ignominiously through Scotland, the Dundonians were reported as having showed him great sympathy, even providing him with clothes.

The most dramatic change to the town's physical appearance as a result of Montrose's raid must have been the separation of steeple and town churches, but the town did not suffer only war damage in those years. One of the periodic attacks of plague or typhus also affected the whole country including Dundee during 1644 and 1645. The Council had even refused to allow the clerk to go to Berwick to join the peace negotiations to try to avoid infection. This was to be the last appearance of the 'pest' in Dundee but that was not known at the time and the disease must have added considerably to the miseries caused by war.

General Monck's Attack

Though so many Scots had taken up arms against Charles I most were horrified when Cromwell had him executed on 30 January 1649. His son was almost immediately recognised as King Charles II in Scotland and was crowned at Scone in January 1651. This eventually brought the Scots into conflict with their erstwhile allies, Cromwell and the English Parliament. Religious divisions weakened the Scots, however, and the English army had a fairly easy time in gaining control of Scotland.

General Monck, however, found himself stopped for a time at Dundee. Local taxes had been imposed to maintain and strengthen the town's fortifications and by July 1651 it was 'in a position of defence'. Ammunition was kept in good order, houses outside the ports were demolished as they had been before Montrose's attack, but they were valued for compensation.

There was enough confidence in Dundee's impregnability among its neighbours for many of them to have lodged their valuables, goods and documents, in the town. On the other hand the Scottish acting government, the Committee of Estates, appears not to have been so sanguine, and it fled from the town when it heard General Monck's army was approaching, only to be captured at Alyth.

On 26 August Monck called on the burgh to surrender but he met with great resistance when his troops began the siege. On 1 September his forces took it by storm. The events of the next couple of weeks reflect no

Birthplace of Anne, Duchess of Monmouth. Used by General Monck as his headquarters, in 1651, after the sack of the burgh. The building stood at the north-west corner of the High Street and south-east of the Overgate until the 1960s.

credit on Monck or the New Model Army and were to have longlasting effects on Dundee. Perhaps it was angry reaction in the English army to the strong resistance put up by the Dundonians that saw the day of looting allowed to Monck's victorious troops lengthen into two dreadful weeks.

By the time they were brought under control it is believed that about one-fifth of the population, regardless of age or sex, had been killed, quite apart from the many casualties that must have occurred among the troops and townspeople in the fierce fighting during the siege. Many of the town's medieval buildings were damaged or destroyed and most of its valuable artefacts and documents were stolen by the rampaging soldiery; as were those deposited there for safety by other towns. Monck's forces are also reputed to have annexed 60 ships that were in the harbour but these were reported to have sunk in the Tay on their way south, filled with spoils of the siege. More Scottish records were lost after the restoration of the Stuarts when the ship returning them sank off Berwick. Dundee's irreplaceable written heritage was thus sadly depleted by English action.

Dundee after Monck

The human loss at the time affected Dundee society deeply and it was many decades before the population or the face of the town recovered completely from this barbarous assault. As will be seen, later population growth was largely made up by incomers. Indeed, it can almost be said that Monck's siege and sack of the town marked the end of medieval Dundee. In 1657 Monck was responsible for another change in the appearance of the town when he ordered that the town walls should be removed, although these were not a medieval relic.

There is no doubt that after the civil wars Dundee slipped considerably down Scotland's urban ladder. In 1656 Richard Franck wrote of 'deplorable' and 'disconsolate' Dundee, but one wonders how much poetic licence he allowed himself. The year before, Thomas Tucker, who surveyed all the Scottish burghs, wrote judiciously that though Dundee through 'her obstinacy' was 'much shaken and abated her former grandeur', yet 'she remayns still, though not glorious, yet not contemptible'. But it was not until the nineteenth century that once again Dundee stood as proudly as it had in medieval and early modern times.

Part II
Restoration to World War One

CHAPTER 7

Trade, Industry and Employment

From Monck to the First Mills, c.1660–1820

Its people 'robbit evin to the sark', Dundee struggled in the second half of the seventeenth century to recover from the ill-effects of the Scottish Revolution. It was difficult though, not only because of the destruction of so many ships and the loss of population, but also due to factors over which Dundonians had no control: the contraction of commerce with France; the demise of Dutch trade and the greater importance of trans-Atlantic links and therefore the west coast ports. Dundee was rapidly losing ground, even though in 1697 the burgh was extended by the purchase of the neighbouring barony of Hilltown, through which ran the main road from Dundee to Forfar.

In the circumstances it seems highly likely that most Dundee traders and manufacturers viewed the prospect of parliamentary union with England as a necessary evil. This is certainly how the nearby burgh of Montrose saw things. Indeed the immediate effect of the Union of 1707 was to reduce further the activity of Dundee's already flat economy. Exposed to more open competition, the town's poor quality linen cloth and woollen plaidings were hard to sell. Parliamentary prohibitions and export duties were additional burdens. Charles Gray, a combmaker, asked the Town Council if he could fill the vacant post of town jailor, largely on the grounds that the Union had 'effectually broke' his business. Although the harbour was marginally busier, this was mainly due to an increase in imports of coal and salt, and ominously as far as the burgh's traders were concerned, more arrivals from England.

The first signs that Dundee was beginning to pull itself out of the slough of post-Union despondency began to appear fairly soon however. The complaint of 19 shipmasters in 1719 that there was no smith capable of doing 'anything aright of shipwork' is an illustration of how bad things had got; that they were trying to persuade the Town Council to allow James Watt, an anchor smith, to set up in the burgh even though he could not afford his burgess fee, reveals that they were anxious to improve them.

Dundee from the west, 1803. The town still retains its medieval appearance, within a rural setting. Within the next two or three decades the pasture land in the foreground was to be swamped by mills and other industrial buildings, although modern street names such as Upper Pleasance hint at the former condition of the district. *St Andrews University Photographic Collection.*

Similarly the merchant George Yeoman was doing his best to encourage his fellow-traders to send better quality linen to the London market. His efforts were underpinned by the establishment in 1727 of the Board of Trustees for Manufactures, a state-aided body which committed itself to improving the Scottish linen industry. Bounty Acts passed by Parliament in 1742 and especially 1745 provided a welcome and powerful stimulus to the export trade in coarse linen cloth. Afterwards the trend in Scottish linen sales was firmly upwards (except for short-term fluctuations). Nowhere was this more so than in Dundee, which between 1746 and 1773 saw a six-fold increase in linen stamped for sale.

The old burgh was clearly recovering something of its former glory: indeed in 1783 the *Dundee Directory* described it as being in a 'very flourishing state', a claim which finds some support in the evidence of new building (to be discussed later)—in addition to the townhouse which the Town Council had felt confident enough to commission the renowned architect William Adam to design in 1731; a fleet of just under 100 sailing vessels; and a range of manufactured products which included linen, sail cloth, cord, thread, stockings, tanned leather and shoes and hats.

Some of these industries were substantial employers of labour. 3,000 people were estimated to have been engaged in thread making for example, which was carried on in various parts of the town, including the Seagate, Overgate and Wellgate. It was here too that most of the town's shoemakers were to be found. Although weavers worked throughout Dundee, they tended to be concentrated in the Hilltown, formerly renowned for its bonnetmakers, while for good reason most butchering was carried on near or on the shore between the beach and St Nicholas Craig, the medieval shambles having been removed from the east end of the High St in mid-century.

However the direct impact of this industrial activity on the town itself was limited in that much of it was carried on outside its boundaries, utilising the water from streams in neighbouring parishes to power machinery and also to boil, clean and bleach yarn and cloth. Within Dundee, sources of running water were limited, and trades such as the waulkers had long been scouring woollen cloth on the upper reaches of the Dighty burn, which in 1804 was serving no fewer than 63 mills, 34 of them within two miles of Dundee. Most were small and not all of them were new: the expansion of the linen trade from the 1730s had encouraged the conversion of several former corn mills for flax processing.

Merchants and merchant-manufacturers, always important in Dundee's history, provided the main human driving force. It was largely on their shoulders that the town's prosperity rested, shipping cloth and other commodities such as grain abroad and importing copper, tar, pitch, deals and luxury items such as fresh and dried fruits, pencils, paper, mirrors and spectacles.

It was some of their number in the later seventeenth and eighteenth centuries who arranged for the collection by their servants of carloads of blankets and other varieties of cloth woven in Dundee for delivery to the outlying waulkmills. Others such as John and William Baxter, of the family which was later to construct the massive linen works at Dens, traded in Russian flax, Dundee's single most important imported commodity. To succeed, flax merchants required fine commercial judgement (about what and when to buy and at what price), a cool head and a great deal of good luck. Once imported, it was sold either to spinners in and around Dundee or spun by merchants on their own account. From 1818, after buying Glamis mill from Patrick Proctor, factor to the Earl of Strathmore, William Baxter was able to spin his own yarn. Later, in 1840, James Buist, who had also traded in flax, acquired Ward Mill from its previous owners, thereby paving the way for the eventual partnership of Don Bros, Buist & Co. The road from merchanting and putting-out to manufacturer was a common one to take. Even more common though, was business failure.

Nevertheless the basis for Dundee's future prosperity was being laid in the eighteenth century. Growth however was slow and in comparative terms the record was modest rather than impressive. Indeed in terms of exports the town was losing ground, accounting for 3.4 per cent of Scotland's export tonnage in the early 1760s but only 0.7 per cent two decades later, when on average only 584 tons per annum were being shipped overseas. Indicative too is the fact that population growth in manufacturing towns elsewhere in Scotland was much more rapid.

This however was to change, remarkably quickly. Just as in Lancashire the advent of steam-powered cotton spinning led to a rush of mill building in towns such as Manchester and Preston, so in flax-spinning steam technology was vital to the transformation of Dundee into one of Scotland's leading industrial towns. Of the four big Scottish Victorian cities, Dundee was the most heavily committed to manufacturing.

There was a distinct quickening in the pace of economic activity during the Napoleonic Wars, which intensified demand for sail cloth, hammocks and cheap shirtings. As a result, imports of flax and hemp to Dundee between 1789 and 1815–19 more than tripled. The great transition however took place in the 1820s, some 40 years later than Paisley or the mill spinning districts of Glasgow.

Changing Gear

Although steam, in the form of a Boulton and Watt 'sun and planet' engine, had been used to drive a flax spinning mill in Guthrie St in the 1790s, and was adopted at a further four mills before 1806, a series of technical difficulties delayed its introduction on a wider scale. Not the least of these was that machine-makers and parts had to be brought north from Leeds, owing to the absence of the requisite skills in Dundee. Unfamiliarity with the new technology and over-ambition on the part of the mill proprietors caused the machines to be run too fast, the fibres to become more brittle, and frequent stoppages resulted.

Suitably compliant labour was scarce: the female domestic spinners of Forfarshire, whose livelihoods and lifestyles were under attack, are reputed to have threatened to set the earliest mills on fire. During the 1820s the male flax hecklers, who prepared the flax by hand for spinning by separating the fibres, combined to fight a well-organised and stout

Ship's master's receipt for four bales of linen, 21 November 1811. During the eighteenth century, growing quantities of linen cloth were shipped from Dundee. Much went to London (in this case to Down's Wharf, on a vessel belonging to the Dundee & Perth Shipping Co), from where it was sent to the Plantations, to be used to clothe slaves. *University of Dundee Archives.*

campaign to maintain their control over the trade and against the introduction of heckling machines—a variety of which was reputed to have
been used in the rival Leeds flax trade since 1809. Powerloom weaving
too was slow to arrive, perhaps because of fears of machine-breaking. For
mill work, employers had to turn to vagrants and paupers, including
poorhouse children, and the infirm, but they were said to be 'lax in their
notion as to regular attendance and good service'. A new work regime
therefore had to be introduced by mill owners such as William Brown of
East Mill, who advised his neighbours to keep the gates and doors of their
works closed in order to keep out 'strollers' and others who would distract
the spinners. Those who stepped out of line were fined, and in the early
years when hours of work were unbearably long and mistakes more likely
to be made or boredom to set in, they might be whipped or beaten.

By various means the hurdles were overcome, with, for example, the
establishment in Dundee of a number of companies of textile machinery
engineers such as Messrs Meldrum & Archibald and J & C Carmichael.
Later the largest textile firms set up and maintained their own foundries
and engineering shops. Between 1827 and 1834 the hecklers' combination was broken. The larger body of hand-workers, the 4–5,000 handloom
weavers of linen who worked for some 400 'manufacturers', found that
they too were unable to resist the incursion of steam power, and in 1836
David Baxter built and set going a powerloom weaving factory, 'looked
upon as one of the wonders of Dundee'. Females were employed in place
of the males who had dominated the handloom sector, and indeed in 1842,
exploiting to the full the fact that unemployment was rife in Dundee,
Baxters's engineer-manager, Peter Carmichael, uncompromising in his
efforts to improve labour productivity, successfully introduced double-
loom working.

The breakthrough can be seen in the number of new mills, which rose
in a series of waves—10 between 1818 and 1822, and a further substantial
advance between 1828 and 1836, when the foundations of many of the
bigger works were laid, including A & D Edward's 'Coffin' mill (so-
called because of its shape), Logie, Tay and Wallace Craigie Works. At
least 30 new mills were built between 1811 and 1835, more in the later
1840s and early 1850s, when work commenced at the Cox brothers'
Camperdown Works in Lochee, where over 5,000 people would eventually be employed, and David Thomson's Seafield Works on a site between
Shepherd's Loan and Taylor's Lane off Perth Rd. Major extensions were
also added at the Baxters's Dens Works. Imports of coal, to fuel the steam
engines, for the gasworks opened in Peep O' Day Lane in 1826, a sugar

refinery and whale blubber boiling, as well as for household purposes, saw a phenomenal five-fold increase between 1820 and 1840. Naturally, demand for flax rose too, with imports increasing ten-fold between 1815–19 and 1845–49. By 1826 Dundee had overtaken Hull as Britain's premier flax port.

Expansion though was far from smooth and as will be seen later periodic downturns in the linen trade caused widespread suffering in Dundee. The Napoleonic blockade in 1807 for example closed the Baltic and caused the price of a ton of flax to rise from £40 to £170. Soon, wrote Charles Mackie, a mill manager who lived through the period, most works closed, 'some of the spinners were put up in the Prison', while others fled from their creditors. Further severe dips in trade were suffered in 1826, 1837, 1842 and 1847.

In the first three-quarters of the nineteenth century though, it is the booms which catch the eye. The Crimean War, the US Civil War and the Franco-Prussian War all encouraged further mill and factory building as wartime demand rocketed for goods such as horse blankets and nose bags, gun and wagon covers, sandbags and sails. 'Better than a gold mine' is how Peter Carmichael described Dens Works. Carmichael though earned less that Baxter Bros' senior partner, Sir David Baxter, who between 1860 and 1869 derived an income of almost £600,000 from the firm. Fortunes were made and Dundee's textile princes were proud of their achievements. Works which had been uniformly functional had added to them classical pediments and Italianate bell towers.

Camperdown's massive soaring campanile chimney, added by James Maclaren in 1865–6 at a cost of £6,000—now virtually alone on a skyline which was once punctuated by a forest of 200 chimneys of all shapes and sizes—was 'the definitive statement of the Cox dynasty', which others tried and failed to match, although the 218' polychrome stack, topped by a cast-iron crown, at Logie Works in Edward St came respectably close.

The declaration of success through size and awareness of current tastes in art and architecture (then greatly influenced by John Ruskin's *The Stones of Venice*) was an important matter. Hence the 'monster pediment' above the Gilroys's Tay Works (completed in 1865 and probably the longest textile mill in Britain) in which amongst the elaborate carving were to be found the first letters of the Christian names of the three partners, along with those from the surname Gilroy. Names and associations could be signified in different ways: the great Manhattan Works at Clepington, opened on a 24-acre site in 1874, were so named to celebrate Dundee's important New York (Manhattan Island) trading connection.

Changing Horses:Linen to Jute c.1820–1914

Manhattan Works was entirely devoted to the spinning and manufacture of jute. By the 1870s linen, Dundee's staple, had passed its peak, even though in volume terms Baxters had become the world's largest flax firm, overtaking the former leader, Marshalls of Leeds. In the heavier end of the trade, where Dundee firms had specialised (unlike Belfast, which concentrated on finer linens) in the manufacture of cloth, foreign competition was intense, tariff walls were being erected, and former markets such as France and Germany simply disappeared. Yarns, once major exports, were being imported into Forfarshire by the end of the nineteenth century, with the result that several mills ceased spinning. More and more the survival of firms such as Baxters or Don Bros, Buist & Co, of Ward Mills in Dundee but who also had works in Forfar, came to depend either on government orders for their heavier varieties of cloth, notably linen duck which the army used for tents, sales of specialist linen cloth, or their willingness to move into jute.

Jute was the 'heartbeat' of Dundee's nineteenth century economy. The fibre had first been imported into Britain in 1791 by the East India Company, but attracted little interest. It was even more difficult to spin than flax and hemp, although it was probably used with other fibres in sacking and bagging made in Dundee in the 1820s. This was done discreetly though, and on a small scale.

The reasons for this are fairly clear: until 1823 linen cloth for sale had to be approved by stampmasters appointed by the Board of Trustees. Dundee's stampmaster, David Blair, 'a man of considerable integrity and influence', refused to pass adulterated or inadequate cloth. Secondly, purchasers of sacking were unwilling to buy anything which they thought had jute in it, as the use of a previous substitute for Baltic hemp, sunn hemp, had weakened the fabric. Thirdly, there was the problem, already referred to, of spinning it.

Yet there is a sense in which the widespread use of jute in Dundee was inevitable. As world trade expanded, so too did demand for bagging and sacking for corn, wool, fertilisers and other bulk commodities; sailing ships required vast yardages of canvas; tents and tarpaulins were needed too—for the new gold mines opening in Australia for example—while jute could be used for carpet backing as well as for colourful carpeting in its own right. Later it was used by Nairns of Kirkcaldy and others who were making a new type of floor-covering, linoleum. Dundee had long been a producer of the coarser and cheaper grades of linen cloth such as osnaburgs, the manufacture of which had been introduced to Scotland from Germany in 1738. And despite the efforts of men such as David Blair, the quality of Dundee goods was not always high. The Forfar linen merchant William Don was always anxious that the bales he sent to London via Dundee should not be confused with cloth made in Dundee, where he sent only his 'inferior' material.

In 1823 the system of stamping cloth was abolished, while in 1832 manufacturers were forced to look at ways of reducing their costs when the long-standing duties on coarse linen cloth exports were removed. It was a search which had been begun earlier by men such as John Maberley, MP for Rye and later Abington, who had come to Scotland in order to make linen more cheaply than he could in England. The advantage of jute was not only that it was extremely strong (in spite of initial fears to the contrary) and durable, it was also considerably cheaper than either flax or hemp. The technical problem of spinning jute was overcome by 'batching' or soaking it with copious quantities of water and whale oil, much to the relief of the town's whalers, who with the introduction of gas lighting to Dundee in the later 1820s, desperately needed a new market.

Precisely who should be given the credit for first importing jute into Dundee, or for using it, is not clear. A London merchant who despatched jute north to Dundee in the early 1820s appears to have been A B Anderson, while his brother William Anderson, a coarse linen manufacturer, had some jute spun. Possibly he had been influenced by John Maberley, for whom he had woven a quantity of canvas. Another early supporter of jute was Hugh Lyon Playfair, son of the Principal of the University of St Andrews and an officer in the East India Company's Bengal Army, who returned from India in 1820—and coincidentally or otherwise, invested in William Halley's Wallace Craigie jute works. The Dundee merchant Thomas Neish was also in near the start, and managed to persuade Bell and Balfour of Chapelshade Works, and around 1832 their successors Balfour and Meldrum, to buy and spin jute yarn. Greater progress, though indirectly as well as directly, was made by James Watt, who teased and carded the jute he was trying to sell, and attracted the interest of John Halley (founder of the present day company of William Halley & Sons Ltd) and William Boyack of South Dudhope Mill. Bankrupted in 1841, Boyack was forced to sell his mill to Robert Gilroy, founder of what was to be the world's second largest jute firm.

The biggest, Cox's, in the person of Henry Cox, first became interested in the possibilities of jute in 1833. Manufacturers of cheap linen and woollen carpetings, sacking and bedding materials, the three Cox brothers were soon convinced of its virtues. Working in the cheaper end of the textile trade, they would do well only if they managed to buy their raw materials at the lowest possible prices and concentrate on volume production. Jute was a business where 1/96 of a penny could make a difference to a deal. Accordingly, from 1845, the firm of Cox Bros (founded 1841) began to replace its army of handloom weavers with powerloom workers. Other handloom factories such as Mid Wynd and Ashton were converted for powerloom working in the 1850s, and greatly expanded in the 1870s.

'Juteopolis' had been born. In 1841 2,570 tons of jute were imported in Dundee; by 1851 this had increased almost seven-fold, to 16,928 tons. Six years later, just after the end of the Crimean War, the figure was 36,554 tons. Thereafter imports soared to reach their peak in 1902 when over 414,500 tons of baled jute were brought into the Tay: 'It was a great sight', wrote one contemporary, 'when the beautiful four-masted sailing ships arrived with jute from India, in that hey-day of Dundee's prosperity.'

'Juteopolis' and the Emergence of Calcutta Competition

Rapidly rising imports however tell only part of the story. They conceal the fact that competitive pressures were growing, primarily from Calcutta, and that the boom in jute was fairly short-lived. (It is cruelly ironic that the emergence of the modern Calcutta industry after 1855 owed a great deal to the skills and abilities of Dundee mechanics and overseers.) The profit levels of the 1860s were never again matched as market after market turned elsewhere for their jute requirements, until by the end of the century Dundee's jute producers could depend on selling large quantities only in the home market and to Latin America and the United States, although even here Calcutta cloth was edging its way in.

This is not to say that the industry was on its last legs. Far from it. On the other hand trade could be dull for long periods and the fight to maintain markets became a deadly serious matter. Closure was the alternative—as nine firms discovered to their cost in 1876 alone. New mills and factories continued to be built and extensions added, but apart from Bowbridge (completed in 1885), there were few more concessions to architectural flamboyance; from the mid-1870s on the emphasis was on cost-cutting and efficiency gains. One way that these were achieved was by adopting the shed principle—as opposed to the multi-storey mill. One of the first was Stobswell Works, completed around 1865 by John Laing and William Sandeman, of Luncarty Bleachfield. The biggest, and one of the most advanced textile works in the country by 1890, was Caldrum Works, designed by Robertson and Orchar of Wallace Foundry for Harry Walker & Sons. Building on this scale however tended to be confined to the few larger companies which had access to the necessary capital. Even they added little that was new after 1900. Inside them however efforts to improve performance carried on, with the older beam engines being replaced by more efficient vertical triple expansion marine engines, and after they had first been installed at Hillbank Linen Works, electric drives. Ironically, the jute industry's survival owed much too to the improved quality of its product, thereby enabling it to hold its own in tarpaulins, pocketings, fine hessians and floorcloth.

Dundee's Economy: Life Beyond Jute?

Dundee's business enterprise was not entirely confined to jute however, and as will be seen in subsequent Chapters, shipbuilding, engineering and whaling were important components of the town's industrial structure, and between them employed some 7,000 men and boys in 1901. It was in works such as Gourlay Bros' Dundee Foundry (established in 1790 as the Dundee Foundry Co) that Dundee's labour aristocrats were to be found, with time-served men such as boilermakers and moulders earning well over 35s. a week, three times as much as the average spinner.

Another notable industry was transport, which employed over 6,000 workers (mainly men) at the turn of the century. Before the appearance of the railways, goods which were to be transported any distance went either by sea or inland carrier. Between 1805 and 1850 the number of vessels at Dundee rose from 138 to 339. Although the number of ship-owners was small (only 95 owners and agents are listed for 1821), between them they employed several thousand men. Whalers for example carried crews of 50-plus; brigs, the most common type of vessel on the coastal routes, had crews of around seven. In the early 1830s there were some 140 inland carriers working on local roads in and out of Dundee, travelling to towns such as Forfar and Kirriemuir.

There were national carriers too, such as Messrs J & P Cameron, whose long strings of horse-drawn waggons created further employment for blacksmiths and farriers, as well as hotel staff in the premises of the major departure and arrival points such as Thomas Moodie's hostelry in Hood's

Close, near the Murraygate. Although the coming of the railways squeezed out the carriers (and eventually most of the passenger traffic of coastal shipping companies such as the Dundee, Perth and London Shipping Company), such losses of employment that resulted were more than compensated for by the demands of the Caledonian and North British railway companies. Both had a major presence in Dundee, and required the services not only of relatively well-paid engine-drivers and guards, but also stokers, shunters, labourers and a small army of porters. The Dundee and District Tramway Co, which began operating in 1877, created further work for drivers and conductors both of horse- and steam-powered trams, until electrification got under way in 1899.

Smaller, but nevertheless noteworthy, was Dundee's printing and publishing industry. In 1825 John Valentine started business making engraved wooden blocks for printing on linen, although it was his son James and grandson William who took the firm into pictorial work. With the ending of the government monopoly on postcards in 1894 and from 1897 the freedom to print or write on the reverse side, Valentines with their collotype printers were in a position to take a commanding lead in the mass-produced postcard business. Until the McKinlay tariff was imposed in 1910, the company sold literally millions of cards in the United States.

Newspapers and periodicals had been published in the eighteenth century, although none survived more than a few years. The pattern continued into the 1800s, with the fearsome sounding *Dundee Protestant Guardian: Or, An Attempt to Expose Some of the Principal Errors and Practices of the Romish Church* for example appearing only in 1829 and 1830. The lives of others were even shorter. In 1801 however the *Dundee Advertiser* was launched, followed by the Conservative *Courier*, which in 1866 became the first half-penny daily paper in the country. The former was purchased by (Sir) John Leng, a Yorkshireman and supporter of a host of radical causes, whose list of titles later included the *People's Journal* (1858), Scotland's first 'national' newspaper, with weekly sales of 250,000 by 1914, the *People's Friend* (1869), and the *Evening Telegraph* (1877). From 1906 however, the year of Leng's death, his publishing empire based in Bank St was to be increasingly under the control of William Thomson, a shipping magnate who had been acquiring various interests in printing and publishing (including the *Courier* in 1886), and his two sons, Frederick and David Couper. Men of remarkable business acumen, they were conscious that amongst the female working classes in particular there was an unsatisfied demand for romance and neo-Gothic horror, and anxious to steer them away from the perils of socialism, they produced a series of easy to digest publications such as *Weekly Welcome*, *Red Letter* and *My Weekly* (which is still in circulation). The radical character of Leng's titles was replaced by the distinctive and immensely popular kailyard-inspired characteristics of D C Thomson & Co.

There was then in nineteenth and early twentieth century Dundee a wide range of industries and occupations. Yet in virtually every case, the employment they generated was significantly less than in any of the other Scottish towns. Popularly, Dundee is known as the town of 'Jute, Jam and Journalism'. Yet printing and publishing employed a smaller proportion of the industrial workforce in Dundee in 1911 than either Glasgow, Edinburgh or Aberdeen. The same could be said of food, drink and tobacco, even though at the end of Queen Victoria's reign the confectionary trade was 'the chief employment for women and girls in Dundee outside the jute mills' (and domestic service). Both were growing in importance, but the fact is that on the eve of the First World War, Dundee was almost as dependent on jute as it had been in the triumphant mid-Victorian decades. If the heartbeat faltered, Dundee would fall.

CHAPTER 8

Dundee and the Sea

The Harbour and Maritime Trade

Dundee's main artery was the Tay, to which it was connected by the harbour. From the earliest recorded times Dundee has been a commercial port, serving both coastal and foreign trade. Although long challenged by Perth, by the middle of the eighteenth century Dundee had emerged as Tayside's pre-eminent port—a position it has never since relinquished.

The most obvious reason for this has been Dundee's geographic location. 'The situation of Dundee upon a salubrious and pleasant southern declivity', noted Dundee's Victorian historian Alexander Maxwell in 1884, 'has the special advantage of being beside a sheltered reach of a noble navigable river.' Maxwell exaggerated. In fact Dundee's position on the north side of the Tay estuary was far from ideal—the deep water channel was on the south side of the river, and the harbour has always been bedevilled with problems of silting.

Other factors were more positive. First amongst them has been the rise of the textile industry, with its substantial and increasing imports of raw materials and exports of the finished products. The development of inland communications—turnpike roads and railways—linked the port to the fertile agricultural hinterland of Strathmore and the outlying towns of Angus and Forfarshire. As the harbour was extended in the later eighteenth and nineteenth centuries to meet the demands of the rising textile trade, the activities it supported grew to meet the needs of other important enterprises—most notably shipbuilding and repairing and whaling.

Yet Dundee's ascendancy as a port was no foregone conclusion. In the mid-fifteenth century it had been declared so unsafe, 'that heavy and untold losses and shipwrecks threatened to befall'. Even the harbour construction undertaken with the revenues authorised by James II in 1447 was judged by Maxwell to be 'not of great extent'. Yet as has been seen, in the sixteenth and early seventeenth centuries Dundee's trade had increased markedly, which necessitated further improvements at the harbour. Indeed in Auchterlonie's *A Description of the Shire of Forfar*, written around 1682, Dundee is described as having 'a good shore, well built with hewn stone, with a key on both sides whereof they load and unload their ships, with a great house on the shore called the packhouse.' Although Auchterlonie was impressed by the scale of Dundee's Dutch and Baltic trade, all the indications are that by the end of the century the harbour was an under-used asset.

The Revival of Maritime Trade

In Chapter 7 it was suggested that the improvement in Dundee's economy, and therefore in the volume and value of her maritime trade, may have begun around 1720. If linen provided the key to this partial return to prosperity, the harbour was the lock, for it was the availability of water transport which enabled the industry to grow.

Although some flax was grown in Scotland, most flax—along with hemp—had to be imported by sea, from northern Russia. Linen cloth, not only from Dundee itself, but also the other Angus textile towns, was shipped from the harbour to London merchants or directly to customers overseas: in the second half of the eighteenth century the volume of outward trade more or less tripled, while coastal shipments increased by a factor of seven.

Harbour Improvements

Obviously the great increase in trade put the port and its facilities under great pressure. In 1730 the Town Council obtained an Act of Parliament authorising it to levy a tax of two pennies Scots on every pint of ale or beer sold in the town, the proceeds to be used to pay off the town debt and repair the harbour, described in the preamble to the Act as being unsafe, due to silting and the decayed state of the piers. By 1736 the Council had set up a specialist committee to consider a plan for the refurbishment of the harbour at a cost of £1,750—a programme which was put into effect gradually over a number of years. By 1759 a contemporary could remark that 'Dundee is one of the best ports for trade in all Scotland.'

But port facilities deemed adequate in 1759 had, by the beginning of the nineteenth century, become totally inadequate. The harbour, commented the *Independent* in 1816,

Dundee's harbour in 1790 was composed of a few quays and breakwaters, and was therefore tidal—work on the sluice-controlled 'wet docks' would have to wait for another thirty-five years. *Dundee Art Galleries and Museums.*

'had been originally constructed on no original plan, but consisted of a series of patchings, stuck together without science or taste. Its quays were becoming ruinous; its depth was diminishing; and it was too small for accommodating the increased shipping of the town.'

The long established practice of misapplying the shore dues, intended in large part for the upkeep of the port, to pay the debts of the town, meant that there was no money to fund the extensive improvements made necessary by the town's policy of 'patching' rather than replacing.

Stevenson and Telford

By this time it had become generally agreed that substantial improvements would have to be made to upgrade what was still a purely tidal harbour. Provost Andrew Riddoch, the controversial but effective ruler of Dundee for nearly 30 years, commissioned one of the leading civil engineers of the day, Robert Stevenson, to submit proposals for extending and modernising the harbour. Stevenson did so, stressing that he had found the existing harbour 'extremely incommodious, and but ill-adapted to the thriving and extensive trade of Dundee.' The major problem was that of silting—no new problem, but becoming more serious as the draught of ships increased. The principal recommendations of Stevenson's report were to turn the existing upper harbour into a wet dock controlled by sluices, and to improve landward access to the harbour area. In the longer term, a second wet dock should be constructed.

Plans to improve the harbour, however, became embroiled in the political infighting of the day. In his long reign over the affairs of the town Riddoch had made enemies, both among the old-established merchant class located in and around the Cowgate, and, latterly amongst a new allegedly 'radical' group of business rivals who were jealous of the power of the Riddoch-dominated Town Council, and who were ready to claim that he had used his position for personal profit. The Stevenson scheme involved the development of an area in which Riddoch held land, and there was opposition to it both on that account, and because control of the harbour would remain in the hands of the Town Council. Riddoch's opponents therefore commissioned a new set of proposals from an equally distinguished engineer—Thomas Telford—with specific instructions to ignore all private property interests. Telford's plan, in its original form at least, was even more ambitious than Stevenson's, but likewise advocated the construction of a wet dock in place of the existing tidal harbour. Under strong pressure from the Council though, Telford agreed to modify his plans.

Battle between the rival groups was soon joined over the legislation proposed for putting the harbour improvement plans into operation. The Council backed scheme would have created a new body of harbour commissioners to take responsibility for the project, but a body dominated by council members. This scheme was vigorously opposed by the merchants on a number of grounds. The plans for improvement were insufficiently detailed; existing property rights were too heavily protected; part of the money to be raised for the scheme was to be used to pay off the town's general creditors; there was insufficient representation on the proposed commission of the groups most interested in the improvement of the harbour.

The Harbour Commission

The upshot of all this wrangling was a new Act passed in 1815, which for the first time vested responsibility for the harbour in a Commission on which the Council held only a minority representation, but which was required to return the harbour to council control after twenty-one years. Chronically short of money (so much so that it nearly abandoned its work in 1821) the Commission's most significant achievement was the creation of Dundee's first wet dock—King William the Fourth Dock, completed in 1825.

Pressure for further development of the harbour and its facilities, however, continued to mount. At the height of the season there was not enough room in the new wet dock for all the incoming flax carrying ships, and none at all for the growing numbers of ships bringing in coal to fuel the steam engines now being introduced into the mills of Dundee in ever larger numbers. In 1829 the *Advertiser* complained that

'Our Harbour has of late been so crowded with shipping, the vessels have been detained for weeks before they could get berths to be delivered in. Instead of being premature in proposing to erect a new wet dock, we suspect that the Commissioners have been too tardy. If the trade goes on increasing as it has done within the last few years the greatest inconvenience and annoyance must be suffered by our shipping long before a new dock can be erected.'

New legislation was required, and in 1830 the Dundee Harbour Commission was replaced by the Dundee Harbour Trust—to control the harbour in perpetuity. Further significant developments followed—notably the completion of a second wet dock, the Earl Grey Dock, in 1834, and the start of work on a third, later to be called the Victoria Dock.

By 1836 the *Advertiser* had dropped its carping tone to rejoice in the work being done to extend the harbour—'additional railroads are in contemplation to connect it more closely with the surrounding districts—new and extensive works are building—and the demand for our staple manufactures is advancing.' In point of fact pressure on the port facilities was already easing off as the boom in the linen trade of the twenties and thirties began to slacken. To begin with work went ahead only slowly, until the new impetus given to the region's textile industry by the Crimean War and the Civil War in the United States brought a new urgency to the project. In 1865 Camperdown Dock was completed, but was soon found to be inadequate to meet the demands of the direct trade with Calcutta. The decision was taken to complete the work on the Victoria Dock begun in the 1830s, and build a new 500 foot graving dock with access from Victoria. The double opening on 16 August, 1875, according to the Weekly News, ranked as one of 'the great events of the history of Dundee'. At the opening ceremony the dignitaries were welcomed by a crowd of 40–50,000 spectators and a guard of honour from the Dundee Artillery Volunteers under Captain Cox. Led by Lord Strathmore, they embarked on the Tay ferry *Dundee* for a short trip on the river, while at separate ceremonies four new ships were launched one after the other from the yards of Thompson's, Gourlay's, the Tay Shipbuilding Company, and Brown and Simpson's. When on its return the *Dundee* entered the Dock, the land around it appeared to be 'completely covered with a sea of human heads, while some of the vessels in the dock were so crowded they listed over with the top-weight'. But nobody was hurt, and at half past four the ceremony ended and they all went home.

Shipbuilding

The interconnection between Dundee's textile industry and the development of harbour facilities in the eighteenth and nineteenth centuries is clear. But of course the harbour and waterfront area had other functions besides those of serving the needs of linen and jute. The most important of these were shipbuilding and whaling, two industries which were also remarkable for the degree of their interdependence.

Much of the stimulus for shipbuilding in Dundee came from the needs of local industry for waterborne transport, and many of the orders for ships came from local shipowners and shipping companies. Before the Napoleonic Wars the Dundee fleet was confined to coastal craft and those engaged in the Baltic and European trades, but after about 1825, when industry was sufficiently productive to make direct shipments to the United States economic, the demand grew for larger ocean going vessels. While some shipowners continued to be small scale—sole owners or shared ownership by local small investors—the period also saw the rise of shipping companies of which one of the most successful was the long-lived Dundee, Perth and London Shipping Company, established in 1826 from the amalgamation of two existing rival companies. The D P & L began with a fleet of 23 ships and capitalisation of £38,000—by 1914 this figure has risen to £280,000.

Shipbuilding—the Early Years

Although some shipbuilding may have been undertaken in earlier times, the history of the industry as an important and continuous activity in Dundee really dates from the later years of the eighteenth century. In *A General Description of the East Coast of Scotland*, published in 1782, there is a brief reference to a dock and a shipbuilder's yard 'where a great deal of business is done', and by 1793 the yard had sufficient work for two masters and 31 journeymen and apprentices. In 1799 'Mr Smith's Dockyard' launched the sloop *Lord Duncan* for the Dundee Shipping Company, and there were at least half a dozen different yards operating in the old waterfront area from Yeaman Shore in the west along the line of modern Dock Street in the first 30 years of the nineteenth century. The Livie family were building boats there from about 1815, as was John Calman. In 1823 a 'Mr Brown of Perth' acquired a Dundee yard, and six years later Thomas Adamson set up his yard in the Seagate.

In 1826 there was attempted a remarkable experiment in co-operative production by the New Shipwright Building Company of Dundee. This venture followed on from a dispute between members of the Dundee Shipwrights Union and their employers over forced reductions in wages and the employment of apprentices. After a strike by ships carpenters the employers ordered them to remove their tools and leave the yard, to which the shipwrights responded by setting up on their own account. The company survived, however, only until 1831. Interestingly a very similar enterprise was embarked upon in almost identical circumstances in 1847, when as Alexander Stephen noted in his diary, 'about 15 of the Union Carpenters commenced shipbuilding, called the Tay Shipbuilding Co.' The company was still operating in 1851.

As we have seen, the early decades of the century were not only a period of expansion of shipbuilding in Dundee, but also a period in which the harbour underwent significant reorganisation. One effect of the construction of the new Earl Grey and King William the Fourth docks was to cut off the old yards from access to the river, forcing them to disperse and relocate to the west and to the east. Contemporary maps show how, while some new yards were positioned alongside the new docks, Calman's and Carmichael's were to be found far up river near the modern railway bridge, and there were three yards further down the estuary at Broughty Ferry—two belonging to Thomas Adamson and one to Peter Borrie.

New Technology

At the same time as these changes were taking place in the physical layout of the docks and the location of the shipbuilding yards, the industry in Dundee was undergoing important technological change. One of the most important aspects of this was the introduction of steam power, the first Dundee ship to be fitted with a steam engine being *The Tay*, built by James Smart in 1814 for the passenger service operating between Dundee and Perth. In the same year Smart's built another steam powered ship, the *Caledonia*, and these were followed by a host of small steamers, mostly coastal craft or river ferries. Dundee's early and successful entry into the construction of steam powered ships was due in part to the existence in the city of an advanced and enterprising mechanical engineering industry. There were several good examples of this, two outstanding firms being J and C Carmichael and the Dundee Foundry. Carmichael's were early associated with the construction of iron steamers, three of which, the *Caledonia*, the *Queen* and the *Tinker* were all built about 1838, before the firm decided to specialise in textile engineering. In 1821 the Dundee Foundry supplied Carmichael's with castings for the engines of the ferryboat *Union*, and had embarked on their long association with maritime engineering in Dundee.

Another important factor in the early and rapid development of steam power in Dundee built ships was the encouragement given by local ship owners and ferry operators, who at this time provided the bulk of the orders for the Dundee yards. The names of some of the local lines of the 1820s and 1830s reflect the growing interest in steam power—the Tay Steam Packet Company, the Dundee and Hull Steam Packet Company, the Dundee and Leith Steam Packet Company. The D P & L, after a long and careful investigation of the merits of steam power, ordered their first steam tug, the *Sir William Wallace*, from the Dundee Foundry in 1829 at a cost of £1,200. Their next two steamers, the coasters *Dundee* and *Perth*, were built in Glasgow, but the Foundry and its successor Gourlay's built the bulk of the D P & L's fleet in the nineteenth century. The first steam ferry across the Tay was the *Union*, mentioned above. She went into service between Dundee and the Fife ports of Woodhaven and Newport in September of 1821. The log book of those first crossings still exists, showing that she made up to 11 crossings a day, six days a week. In calm weather and high water the journey normally took about 20 minutes, but in bad weather and low water, forcing her to skirt the sandbanks, it could take an hour. Another famous steamer, the wooden *Forfarshire*, built by Adamson and Borrie in 1836, was wrecked off the Farne Islands in 1838, some of her passengers being rescued in heroic fashion by Grace Darling and her father James.

The second important technological innovation in this period was the introduction of the iron ship. In Dundee, as we have seen, the first iron steamers were built by Carmichael's around 1838. For a time iron ship-building was carried on by Peter Borrie, both on his own account at the Broughty Ferry yard, and in association with Thomas Adamson at Dundee. But it would be wrong to assume that there was a neat transition from wood to iron. Indeed for a period of ten years or more after 1842, when Adamson went bankrupt and Borrie, also in financial difficulties, left for the north of England, iron construction of ships in Dundee came to a halt, and the 1850s and 1860s witnessed a late flowering of the wooden sailing ship.

Dundee and her shipbuilders were well placed to play a full part in this development. Despite early involvement in steam power and iron ship construction, the experience of most of Dundee's shipwrights was in wood and sail. The town enjoyed a well deserved reputation for the production of fine sailcloth—Baxter's made the sails for Nelson's *Victory*—and Dundee had long imported timber, so that her yards were less dependent than some of their competitors on home grown supplies of oak.

But the crucial factor in the expansion of wooden sailing ship construction at this time was probably the growth in local demand—principally for whalers and jute carriers.

Largely in response to the demand for whale oil for jute batching, Dundee whaling by the last quarter of the nineteenth century had outstripped its British competitors in the Arctic. One factor in this success was the technical skill and expertise of local yards in this specialised branch of the shipbuilding industry. Whaling ships were required above all else to be strong enough to withstand the pressure of the ice pack, and experience had shown that properly designed and constructed wooden ships were far superior to iron ones in this respect. At the same time there were clear advantages in providing the whaling ships with at least auxiliary steam power, both to shorten the time taken to reach the whaling grounds, but more importantly to enable them to manoeuvre in the crowded waters of the ice floes. In 1857 Stephen's yard first installed an auxiliary steam engine in the *Tay*, and in 1859 launched the *Narwhal*, the first of many auxiliary steam whalers to be designed as such.

Alexander Stephen's Yard

The association between the Alexander Stephen shipbuilding company and Dundee whaling was long and close. The company established itself in Dundee in the mid-1840s, joining the few survivors of the industrial depression, the Calmans and Robert Brown. Stephens were not however newcomers to the industry, and had been building wooden ships at a number of locations for the best part of a century. Their latest move had been from Arbroath, where the construction of the Dundee-Arbroath railway had disrupted the local shipyard. At Dundee, on the other hand, they enjoyed the advantages of a site on the newly constructed Marine Parade, the availability of wood and sailcloth supplies, and of course a growing local demand. Their decision to continue to build in traditional materials was clearly not dictated by any unwillingness to innovate. When they first came to Dundee, so the *Advertiser* commented, ships were still being built 'on much the same principles as served Noah'. At the Stephen yard a covered-in berth 180 feet long allowed work to be carried on in bad weather; as we have seen the yard was ready to employ steam power where appropriate; and their commercial interests were widened to include timber importing in their own ships, and direct involvement in the whale and seal products business. In 1894 the Stephen yard built what has been described as 'the greatest sailing ship ever launched on the Tay' —the *Pitlochry* of 3,080 tons. It was not a steady trade however. In 1895 no sailing ships were launched. As the *Dundee Year Book* reported disconsolately, 'the Glory has departed.'

For the Stephen company, the launching of the *Pitlochry* was indeed its swan song as far as building in Dundee was concerned. Long before— as long before as 1850—the firm had acquired a yard on the Clyde at Kelvinhaugh to build iron ships, and in 1869 they bought a second at Linthouse, and left Dundee. Their Dundee yard was handed over to the Dundee Shipbuilders Company, formed largely from the old Stephen workforce and including many of the foremen and staff amongst its shareholders. It was this company which built RRS *Discovery* in 1901. Reconstituted as the Dundee Shipbuilding Company in 1906, the firm finally closed its doors in 1920.

The Dundee Clipper Line

The market for whaling vessels, however, was not the only stimulus to the continuation of wooden ship building in Dundee yards. Prior to 1850, perhaps surprisingly, Dundee's textile manufacturers had seldom invested in the ships which carried their products. In the prosperous years of the American Civil War and after, however, the big jute manufacturers began to see the attractions of owning and operating their own carrying fleets, rather than sharing their profits with London middlemen.

A good example is that of William Cox of Cox Brothers, who had shares in many of the whaling and sealing companies of the day, as well as in the D P & L, of which his son Arthur became chairman. In 1874 William Cox joined with others to form the Dundee Clipper Line, and he was to hold substantial shares in all but one of its fleet of 15 vessels. From the first the directors of the Clipper Line pursued a policy of placing orders for ships with the local yards—eight of the first eleven ships owned by the Line were built in Dundee. One of the finest examples of the marque was the *Duntrune*, built by Alexander Stephen and Sons in 1875. Another was the *Maulesden*— named after the palatial mansion near Forfar owned by the Cox's. This ship was built originally as a jute carrier plying between Dundee and India, but in 1883 with 500 emigrants on board she made a record breaking 69 day passage from Greenock to Maryborough in New South Wales.

While the Dundee shipyards benefited to some considerable extent from the patronage of local buyers, the industry could hardly have survived, let alone prospered, on that basis alone. For instance, the demand for whalers was of limited duration, and the *Terra Nova*, built by Stephens in 1884, was the company's last. Such figures as are available suggest that in the last decade of the nineteenth century local orders accounted for only about 14% of the total Dundee tonnage, though this figure conceals the shift from a relatively high percentage to an almost negligible one over the 10 year period. In contrast, other British orders accounted for 57%, and overseas orders for the remainder. The output of the Dundee yards was extremely varied, including fishing boats, light-ships, and ferries, but in terms of tonnage the largest class of ships produced was of boats designed primarily as cargo carriers, often with passenger carrying capability as well.

If the last four decades of the nineteenth century then had witnessed the final flowering of wood and sail building in Dundee, virtually the same period was marked by the rise of iron and steam. In the 1860s the tonnage of wooden ships produced in Dundee yards was almost equalled by that of iron, and almost as many ships were powered by steam as by sail. In 1877 two of the old yards specialising in wood and sail, Brown and Simpson and the original Dundee Shipbuilding Company went out of business, leaving only Stephen's as a yard of any size still turning out wooden ships. The biggest firms in Dundee now were those which built mostly or exclusively in iron.

Gourlay's

The first of these, and for many years the largest, was Gourlay's, founded in 1854. The Gourlays, young sons of an East India Company doctor, became involved in marine engineering works in Dundee by becoming partners in the Dundee Foundry in 1846 and sole owners in 1853. The next year they leased land from the Harbour Trust and opened a shipyard, from the very beginning building exclusively in iron, as well as going for steam and screw propulsion. One of their earliest contracts was to build the *London* for the D P & L, inaugurating a long and mutually beneficial association between the two firms. The *London* was the first screw steamer owned by the D P & L, and was also notable for having been sunk in the Tay off Monifieth in 1865 after a collision with the collier *Harvest Queen*. After a year on the river bed the ship was raised by Henry Gourlay, and, renamed the *Hull* in 1892, continued in the service of the D P & L until 1909.

By the time of the raising of the *London*, Gourlay's had already become the largest of the Dundee yards, both in terms of the size of the workforce (300 men as against 220 at Brown and Simpson's, and 200 at Stephen's), and in terms of output. The company was notable also for its record of technological innovation. Back in 1851, before they went into shipbuilding on their own account, Gourlays supplied a 70 hp. engine for the *Correo*, a screw steamer built by Brown and Simpson. It was the Gourlays who in 1858 installed a steam engine in the wooden whaler *Tay* for the Alexander Stephen Company—a highly successful combination which Stephen's were to use in their whalers again and again. In the same year Gourlays introduced the compound steam engine to Tayside, and in their *Forfarshire* built in 1861 they were amongst the pioneers in the use of steel in ship construction. The *Encyclopedia Britannica* of 1887 used Gourlay marine boilers as illustrations of the 'most modern construction', and in 1905, not long before the yard finally closed, the firm was re-equipping with electricity and taking out a licence to instal Parson's turbine engines. Gourlay's ships were notable also for the quality of their appointments—their steel schooner *London*, built in 1892, boasted a fine music room decorated with scenes from the works of Sir Walter Scott, while the ship was fitted with electric lighting supplied by Lowdens of Dundee.

In 1874 Gourlay's was joined on the Dundee waterfront by W. B. Thomson, a native of Broughty Ferry, who came to shipbuilding, like the Gourlays and later the Pearces, by way of engineering and partnership in a local foundry. In 1867 Thomson took over sole ownership of the Tay Foundry, and in 1874 began to build ships, his first contract being to build a yacht for the Earl of Caledon, after whom the Caledon shipyard was named. Thomson's success was remarkably rapid—within two years his yard was second only to Gourlays in terms of output—and in addition he acquired a yard on the Clyde. In 1888 the company bought out the ailing Pearce Brothers yard, formed only seven years previously, and then in 1896 the business was reconstructed as the Caledon Shipbuilding and Engineering Company, with Thomson as joint managing director. Further contraction of firms engaged in shipbuilding in Dundee came with the demise of Gourlays in 1908 after running into severe financial difficulties partly caused by the cost of re-equipping in 1905. With the closure of the Dundee Shipbuilding Company in 1920, only a single yard—the Caledon—survived into the second quarter of the twentieth century.

Launch of the *City of Winnipeg* at the Caledon yard, October 1955. Despite much investment in modern machinery and production methods, in common with the rest of the British shipbuilding industry, The Caledon struggled to survive in the post-War years, and eventually closed down in 1982. *D C Thomson & Co.*

The Caledon

Although the Caledon shipyard itself is now defunct, much of its history is a story of success—won in defiance of national economic difficulties, and born of managerial foresight and high standards of workmanship. In its early years the company specialised in building fast passenger liners and medium sized passenger cargo boats. During the First World War virtually all production was switched to Admiralty orders, and both the Caledon and the still surviving Dundee Shipbuilding Company were given over almost wholly to naval work, both construction and repair.

Before the war was over, a farsighted management had acquired the lease of a 20 acre plot of land adjacent to its existing yard, on which after the war was constructed a new yard with the most up to date equipment, able to build ships up to 600 feet long. In 1922–23 it launched the *Perseus* and the *Meneleus* for the Blue Funnel Line—the first ships of over 10,000 tons to be launched on the east coast of Scotland. Perhaps the company's greatest triumph was to weather the depression of the early 1930s, managing to survive when so many other British yards foundered. Indeed the 41,000 tons launched in 1930 was a new company record, and even the following year yielded the satisfactory total of nearly 25,000. Over the next three years orders dwindled to almost nothing, but from 1935 business began to pick up until the outbreak of World War Two brought about a vast increase in tonnage—mostly cargo vessels but also some naval craft including one aircraft carrier. In the post war years a second modernisation programme was carried out at the cost of over £1 million, and in 1954 the yard launched the largest vessel ever built on the east coast—the 12,000 ton Norwegian *Storeas*. In the 1960s shipbuilding orders began to fall off in the face of fierce competition from yards in the Far East, although some valuable work was provided in the form of building the box girders for the new Tay road bridge. The Caledon finally went out of business in 1982.

Whaling and Exploration

The connection between shipbuilding and whaling in Dundee has already been established, as has Dundee expertise in this branch of the shipbuilding industry, and this partially explains the dominance of Dundee as a whaling port in the later nineteenth century. But the city's connection with whaling goes back much further than that—some would claim as far back as the twelfth century.

In modern times, the Dundee whaling industry really began with the setting up of the Dundee Whale Fishing Company in 1754. In the 1730s and 1740s the British government became concerned at the country's dependence on foreign supplies of oil, and offered cash bounties of as much as 40 shillings on a ton of whale oil. The effect was to create a whole new industry, initially exclusively English but which later spread to Scotland. The first subsidised Scottish whaling voyage was from Leith in 1750, and the Dundee Whale Fishing Company was not far behind. Their ship, the *Dundee*, sailed almost every year to Greenland, accompanied from time to time in the 1750s and 1760s by the *Grandtully*. In the later years of the century there were four Dundee whalers in regular operation—the *Dundee*, the *Tay*, the *Success*, and the *Rodney*. In 1791 the *Success* caught 11 whales—one of the highest catches in the country.

Whaling traditionally, it seems, declined in times of war—largely because both ships and seamen were commandeered for naval purposes. This had been the effect of the American War of Independence in the 1770s and 1780s and was to occur again during the Napoleonic Wars at the turn of the century. But the end of the hostilities saw the beginning of steady growth in the industry, as well as a shift from the old and almost exhausted fishing grounds off Greenland to the Davis Straits. From 1811 to 1820 Dundee's whaling fleet, with an average of about 10 ships each year, was counted amongst the six largest in the country—on a par with its great Scottish rival, Peterhead. The same period saw the building of oil yards and refineries at what was then the eastern end of the harbour—the only traces left today being in street names like Whale Lane and Baffin St.

From the peak of the 1820s, competition from coal gas for lighting purposes began a decline in whaling, and when ships were lost, as they so often were, they were not replaced. 1830 was one of the most disastrous years in the history of the industry, with 19 ships lost and 21 returned empty out of the UK fleet of 91. 1835 was a bad year too, and in 1836 the ice fields began forming as early as May, trapping six vessels. Not until the following April did three of the missing whalers reappear at Stromness, with reports of great loss of life. The *Thomas*, it appeared, had been crushed in the ice, and the *Advice*, although freed, limped into Sligo with only seven survivors out of a crew of 49. For the next 20 years Dundee whaling operated only on a relatively minor level, while leadership in the UK passed from Hull to Peterhead.

What altered the picture in Dundee in the late 1850s were changes in the local textile industry, and in associated technology. Dundee textile manufacturing, especially jute, was about to enter one of its most profitable periods, as it sought to satisfy the huge demand for coarse fabrics generated by the American Civil War of 1861–65. The increase in the demand for jute led to an increase in demand for whale oil—used in emulsified form to soften the raw jute fibre—and the price of oil quickly rose from £30 to £50. At the same time the steam technology developed to power Dundee's mills and factories began to be applied to ships, including whalers. As we have seen, in the late 1850s the Stephen company had successfully combined steam power with wooden construction in the *Tay* and the *Narwhal* and for the next quarter of a century the company continued to supply the local whaling industry with wooden hulled steamers, a combination which offered great strength to withstand the pressure of the ice, together with speed and manoeuverability in the floe-strewn fishing grounds. The extra speed offered by steam power also made it possible to fit in two trips each year—one in the spring to the

The whaling ship the *Balaena*, whale-boats lashed to its decks, leaving Dundee for the Arctic, late nineteenth century. Although built in Norway, the *Balaena* was one of the last and best-known vessels in the shrinking Dundee whaling fleet. *Valentine Collection, University of St Andrews Archives.*

sealing grounds of Greenland and Newfoundland, and another in the summer to the whale fisheries of the Davis Straits—greatly improving the profitability of the fleet. The size of the ships also increased—the largest being the *Arctic*, 800 tons, launched in 1875. The last steam whaler to be built was the *Terra Nova*, in 1884.

Throughout the 1860s and 1870s Dundee's whaling fleet grew steadily in numbers—eight ships in 1861, 12 in 1867, rising to a peak of 15 or 16 by the mid-1880s. Already, however, the signs were apparent that the industry had only a limited future. Overdependent on demand for oil from the jute trade, the whalers were hard hit by competition from mineral oil for jute batching. Later voyages indeed depended on whalebone rather than oil for their profits—at its peak whalebone for dresses and corsets fetched between £2,000 and £2,500 per ton. In any case the Arctic waters were being hunted out—the focus of activity now was shifting towards the Antarctic. In 1892 a leading Dundee owner, Robert Kinnes, sent his four whalers on an expedition to the Antarctic, but when they returned

Arctic Tannery, early 1900s. William Stephen Sons & Co produced fur and skins from seals and other Arctic animals brought back by the Dundee whaling fleet. The picture is of skins being soaked in lime vats. The outlines of some of these vats are visible in the forecourt of the Royal Naval Reserve, Marine Parade, Dundee. *Dundee Art Galleries & Museums.*

the following summer they brought with them seal oil and skins, but no whale bone. The experiment was not repeated.

Other countries, notably Norway, were to exploit the Antarctic whale fisheries successfully—their success being due in large part to the application of new fishing methods: the exploding harpoon and the factory ship. Dundee owners, once the leaders in the development of the modern whaling ship, were now left behind. By 1913 there were only two whalers still working out of the port, and with the outbreak of the First World War whaling in Dundee was finally abandoned.

RRS Discovery

There is, however, a postscript. In 1901 the Dundee Shipbuilders Company, the inheritors of the Stephens yard and much of its expertise, with

The *Discovery* on her way home to Dundee in 1988, dwarfed by the carrier ship *Mammoet*. *D.C. Thomson & Co.*

great ceremony launched the Antarctic research ship *Discovery*—constructed on exactly the same principles as a regular steam whaler, and the last such vessell to be built in Dundee. Not surprisingly, the launch on 22 March attracted huge crowds which lined Marine Parade.

As an exploration ship *Discovery* fulfilled all expectations, withstanding the pressure of the Antarctic ice for two years without damage. A further link with Dundee's whaling history was provided by the *Terra Nova*, the last whaler to come out of the Stephens yard, and the ship which both brought relief supplies to the *Discovery* expedition in 1904, and carried Captain Scott's final ill-fated expedition to the South Pole in 1910.

After her long career as an exploration and training vessel, in 1985 the decision was taken to bring *Discovery* back to Dundee, where on 22 April 1986 she was welcomed by crowds which rivalled in numbers and enthusiasm those at her launch. Here in Victoria Dock she joined the frigate Unicorn, the oldest British built warship afloat and a denizen of Dundee since 1873. Now being restored by Dundee Industrial Heritage and a major tourist attraction, *Discovery* has become the symbol not only of Dundee's maritime past, but also of her future as the 'City of Discovery'.

CHAPTER 9

Social Life from the Restoration to the Eve of the Age of Jute

Image and Reality

The image of Dundee which was conveyed by some nineteenth century observers is of an urban society which was transformed—for the worse—by the arrival of flax and jute spinning mills, weaving factories and calender works, and the hordes of migrants who were recruited to work in them. Even before the great age of jute though the character of the town was changing: 'Philetus' reported in the *Dundee Magazine* of 1799 that, 'Vice, manufactures and population', had 'kept a steady jog trot together'.

Even so, looking back from the vantage point of the mid-1860s one Dundonian could recall that in the first years of the nineteenth century, by 10 pm the 'Streets of Dundee were as quiet as a country Village Lane'. Although his account was almost certainly coloured by the passage of time, he was not alone in his views. In the light of the reputation Dundee would later acquire for drunkenness, it is notable that in his little-known written reminiscences about Dundee in the 1820s and 1830s John Gray could recall a time when people 'went for refreshment, and being refreshed … went away' from the numerous inns and hotels which were then to be found in the town centre closes. Observations such as these provide a telling contrast to the Circuit Court judge Lord Cockburn's mid-century description of Dundee as a 'sink of atrocity, which no moral flushing seems capable of cleansing'.

Sin, Sex and Social Control

Immorality, outbreaks of public disorder and crime were in evidence in the later seventeenth and eighteenth centuries too, as they had been in the medieval period. The Scottish Reformation had in Dundee lost none of its force where public morality was concerned. Sexual misdemeanours in

Petition from Robert Dickson, the town jailor of Dundee, to the town council, 1720. Dickson is complaining that he has not been paid for looking after a number of prisoners who were incarcerated following the meal riots of February 1720. Amongst those suspected of being involved and who had been imprisoned were 'two of Lachlan Leslie maltman his women servants'. *Dundee Archive and Record Centre.*

particular continued to be frowned upon, as the many women who were accused by the magistrates of being 'whores and strumpets' found to their cost when they were banished from the town, and threatened with being burned on the cheek by the hangman if they returned. There was evidently something of a minor purge on immorality in the financial year 1751–2 when the burgh council paid out £1.4s. 'for Transporting severall Whores to Fyffe'. Although the partners of prostitutes appear to have escaped public censure, some men found their sexual infelicities catching up with them, as in the case of James Rind, servant to a weaver in the Wellgate, who in 1784 was found guilty of fornication with Helen Kay, fined and ordered to pay for the ensuing child's upkeep.

Also commonplace were minor disturbances, such as disputes between neighbours, which in early modern times could involve the use of swords—which tended to be rattled rather than drawn. By the end of the eighteenth century 'Ferrera steel' had been replaced for the purposes of duelling by the pistol.

One of the earliest instances of what can be defined as popular protest took place towards the end of the sixteenth century, when 'several poor tenants of West Ferry and Monifieth' complained collectively to the Privy

Council about the brutal manner in which the Laird of Ballumbie was alleged to have evicted them from their houses. The evidence for crowd action (but not necessarily its incidence) becomes thicker later on: in 1720 for instance, Dundee was one of a number of towns in Fife and Tayside which experienced an unprecedentedly angry bout of food rioting. The house of the merchant George Dempster was sacked while victual was taken from at least one vessel which was lying at the harbour: the mob, led by John Brunton, deacon of the weavers' incorporation, was dispersed only when a detachment of troops arrived from Perth. Several people were arrested, including 'two of Lachlan Leslie maltman his women servants', while during the skirmishing, one man lost his life.

Fatalities however were rare, food riots less so. The inhabitants of east coast ports like Dundee objected to the shipment outwards of grain when local shortages were threatened, or because of suspicions of profiteering on the part of bakers and merchants at a time when medieval trading regulations, which had tended to favour the urban consumer, were being usurped in the interests of producers and free market principles. The riot was a form of community politics, where the unenfranchised seized the opportunity of forcefully reminding their social superiors that the status quo and the crowd's deference were conditional upon them meeting their obligations towards those they ruled. In this and later instances, in 1773, 1792 and 1812, the 'mob' in Dundee was demanding that those in positions of authority act in accordance with a long-established paternalist code and ensure the availability of basic foodstuffs at a fair price. Once the head of steam had been let off and popular demands met, peace would generally prevail once more. It was a scenario which was well understood by Provost Riddoch, who in 1816 could still mingle with the rioters and urge them to return home.

Dundee was changing though and his successors would feel less comfortable about walking freely through its streets and wynds. By 1837 it was felt that a permanent military presence was required. A request from Perth Town Council that troops should be in attendance at the next sitting of the Circuit Court there was turned down by the Secretary of State on the grounds that Dundee's 'large Manufacturing Population' demanded that they remain in Dundee where they were 'more necessary' than at neighbouring Perth.

In the first half of the eighteenth century however, it was the customs and excise officers who felt the full force of what could be remarkably ferocious assaults. Although such attacks had taken place before 1707, the Union of that year, with its raised taxes on a wider range of commodities, signalled the commencement of a campaign of non-compliance throughout much of Scotland. Inspired perhaps by their sympathy for the Stuart cause, but more likely by economic self-interest, Dundee merchants were not averse to raising willing mobs from amongst the ranks of the poor and less prosperous to storm the town's customs warehouse and make off with 'seized' goods such as tobacco, wines and French salt, upon which duties had not been paid.

The officers were frequently subjected to rough beatings, with much 'effusion of blood', even when they were under the protection of soldiers who were marched in to assist them in carrying out their duties in and around the town. Indeed in December 1736 it was reported that 'the Duty of late has been so hard' that the soldiers then stationed in Dundee were 'not able to bear it'. Another company was urgently requested by the local military commander. Little support was forthcoming from the town's authorities who tended to turn a blind eye and were reluctant to bring offenders to justice. Indeed one of Dundee's baillies had in 1735 been accused of illicitly removing the weights used by the customs office and running additional lead into them, thereby attempting to defraud the revenue.

As in the other Scottish towns then, there were more public disturbances than is sometimes assumed. Many though—perhaps most—were instances of pretty low level disorder, such as the stone-throwing skirmishes fought between the boys of the English and Grammar schools and the territorially-based street battles of the youths from the Hilltown and the Murraygate. There were far longer periods of relative calm. It is true that the mood of the less dignified ranks of Dundee's inhabitants was frequently tetchy, and could readily be tempted to make things difficult for the authorities. This was almost certainly the reason why much earlier, in 1604, the town's piper had been ordered to stop playing seditious tunes.

Usually, the magistrates were able to nip potential trouble in the bud. They were quick to fine or even banish petty thieves and other miscreants. Public whipping was another option, though less often used. The indications are that Dundee's five or six lightly-armed officers, often old (but remarkably fit) ex-soldiers dressed in distinctive blue lace-trimmed coats and three-cornered laced hats, could usually be relied upon to maintain order in the streets. Only occasionally did their numbers have to be supplemented, as at what later became known in some quarters as the 'fechtin fairs', Stob's Fair and Lady Fair. Visitors from the surrounding countryside—usually labourers presenting themselves for hire and vendors of cattle and horses—complained (in a petition to Dundee's magistrates in 1813) that the town dwellers were in the habit of kicking them, knocking off their hats, stealing from them and calling them 'countray joks'.

There were also powerful countervailing forces at work, harnessing the emotions and energies of those who might otherwise have been disaffected. The various craft associations exercised considerable authority over their members as well as those who worked for them, determining hours and conditions of work and rates of pay. The masters' control however was not absolute: a combination (trade union) of journeymen wrights was certainly in existence in 1752, when they refused to work after dark. Their protest made little difference: the Dean of Guild insisted that their hours of work had 'always been from 6 am to 8 pm and should remain so'. There is however a suggestion that they had engaged in concerted action as early as 1695, when they 'seduced ilk ane other not to fie with any maister langer than ane week or ane twenty days at maist', whereas their employers preferred to hire them on longer—quarterly, six-monthly or annual—contracts. Even so, the vertical bonds of trade and craft skill and pride were strong, underpinned by practices such as the bulk buying of grain by some trades for sale to their members, and the unity-enhancing splendour of the shoemakers' annual pageant of St Crispin, referred to earlier.

Although not always with the unanimous support of its members, along with its counterparts elsewhere in Scotland, the Town Council each year sponsored a series of displays of loyalty both to the reigning monarch, and after 1707, the newly-created British state. Bells were ordered to be rung and flags raised on numerous occasions deemed worthy of celebration, such as the birthdays of members of the royal family and naval and military victories, thus bringing home to Dundonians the fact of their citizenship of the expanding British empire.

From the time of Charles II's Restoration, the noisiest most colourful day of all was the monarch's birthday. To the bells were added the sound of cannon and small arms fire, while the lighting of great bonfires, fuelled with coal and tar barrels, added to the spectacle and celebratory symbolism of the day. The town's inhabitants were ordered to illuminate their windows, with fines being imposed on those who failed to do so. For the Town Council and their guests as well as the populace it provided a few hours of exuberant release from the drudgery of daily life. Great quantities of liquor were purchased with which to drink loyal toasts; claret, sherry and white wine for the official party, 'dregs' for the crowds at the cross.

The gunners were rewarded with ale. New glasses were specially bought (63 in 1710), as were a variety of foodstuffs which could include bread, tongues, walnuts, oysters and anchovies.

As in late medieval times music was an integral part of this and other festive gatherings. Thus for example the renowned Neil Gow, 'fiddler from Dunkeld', was paid £7.16s. Scots for playing at the ball which was held to celebrate King George III's coronation. Earlier, in August 1713, the civic authorities had expressed their concern about the 'decay' of the town's music school owing to the old age of the current music master, Alexander Keith, and accordingly, John Coupar from Aberdeen was employed in his place. Musical entertainment was by no means confined to the halls and dining rooms of the elite: indeed the widespread popularity of fiddle music is revealed in 1718 in a petition from the town's 'official' musicians—Alex Neilson and George Morrison, 'vilers'—who complained about the numbers of incomers 'from the Cuntry' who were adversely affecting their livelihood by gaining employment by playing dance tunes at weddings in the burgh.

It is notable that the flow was towards Dundee. Indeed it was observed of Dundonians in the early 1800s that their interests were 'largely centred within their own community, which to a great extent was cut off from the outside world'. It would however be wrong to exaggerate this: as has been seen, Dundee had been very much in the mainstream of north European cultural development in the sixteenth century. Despite official disapproval, visiting theatre companies had continued to visit, and performed in Dundee on several occasions in the eighteenth century, bringing with them fashionable plays from the south. When Dundee's first permanent theatre, the Theatre Royal at Yeaman Shore, was opened in 1800, the first public performance was of Shakespeare's *Merchant of Venice*.

Nevertheless, around 1830, while 140 carriers were moving flax, yarn and cloth in and out of Dundee, they were transporting commodities, not people. The mail came and went daily, but letters arrived from London only every three days in 1799. Stage coaches carried 'travellers of every description', but they were hardly numerous; mass travel and the age of the steam locomotive lay in the future. As has been seen, the shipping of the port was increasing, but by and large it was the merchants and leading citizens who looked outwards and over the horizon, less so the growing body of ordinary Dundonians. However even the elite appear to have been less anxious than their counterparts in Edinburgh or Glasgow to plan or import the best architectural practices (although slower economic growth made this more difficult). Yet to refer in this context only to William Adam's Town

The Town House, or 'Pillars', designed by William Adam in 1731, which for a time placed Dundee in the forefront of Scottish municipal building. This late eighteenth century engraving shows a fire pump in action, and may be a portrayal of a fire in 1773 which temporarily endangered the Town House. It survived this and other conflagrations until 1931. *Perth and Kinross District Archives.*

House is to disregard unfairly men such as Samuel Bell, Town Architect, whose work is best seen today in St Andrew's church in King St (1772) and Provost Riddoch's Nethergate mansion (1790, now the Clydesdale Bank), or later eighteenth century buildings such as Annfield House (1795) in Annfield St. And while obviously much less spectacular than Edinburgh's New Town, some refashioning took place in Dundee after c.1760, in the form of street widening and the creation of new streets such as Crichton St in 1783 and Castle St in 1795. Nor were tasteful examples of building styles absent, as can be seen in the neo-classical Exchange Coffee House in Shore Terrace (1828, now Winter's) and several terraces and villas, as at Magdalen

Place (1830s), the High School (1834) and The Vine, in Magdalen Yard Rd (1836), but such developments were to be swamped and made to look disproportionately small as the tentacles of industrialisation prised their way into virtually every nook and cranny of Dundee.

Separating Spheres

The common enthusiasm for fiddle music noted above just hints at a lingering sense of medieval community or 'oneness' in the earlier eighteenth century, although this was fast disappearing, hastened by the devastation wreaked by Monck's army. Class divisions, always there, were becoming harder to bridge and in Dundee as in the much of the rest of urbanising Europe in the eighteenth century, the worlds of polite and popular culture were drawing apart.

Indicative is 'Philetas's' observation of 1799 that 'Spirits and hobgoblins are little known in these days: they flee from society and refinement'. He was referring to the elite: further down the social scale 'freits' (superstitious beliefs) were firmly held long into the next century, in the form of 'ghaists', death warnings, fairies and witches. A different sort of pointer is that while the provost and magistrates still conducted themselves as they had for decades, walking in procession to the East Church every Sunday for example, bedecked in black silk cloaks and cocked hats, they were uncomfortably conscious that they were treated with much less respect by the 'rabble' than they had been formerly. Nevertheless 'genteel' Dundonians could still enjoy a round of balls (or 'Assemblies') during the winter months, and throughout the year a succession of lavish dinners, teas and suppers—the last of which usually ended with games of whist, or for the younger members of the party, cards.

That the mood was changing can also be seen in the way that the monarch's birthday was celebrated. By the end of the eighteenth century the Town Council had begun to withdraw from those activities which were most likely to excite the passions of the watching crowds and lead to serious disorder. The lower classes however were not to be denied what had become at least a partial holiday. There were precious few of these in the first decades of the nineteenth century: apart from Sundays these amounted to two fair days, a day at New Year and the spring and autumn Fast days. The flax hecklers and factory weavers also honoured 'Saint Monday', but they then had to make up time later in the week in order to earn a living wage.

It was however much more than a short break from work. The monarch's birthday had been transformed from a day of formal if boisterous rejoicing into an occasion not only of drunken abandon but also one when the crowd (the 'rifraff' of the town, according to one observer), turned its wrath on Dundee's more prosperous citizens and particularly objectionable local individuals or institutions. Sometimes things could take an extremely serious turn, as in 1838 when James Scott's Pantheon Theatre in Union St was burned to the ground.

However, perceptive observers of popular politics such as Robert Rintoul, editor of the *Dundee Advertiser*, recognised that despite the discomfort felt by the respectable classes, or an outraged mariner correspondent who had been knocked over by an old kettle in the High Street on 4 June 1817, the 'privilege' of the 'rabble ... to be riotous' on the king's birthday was a vital element in the burgh's constitution.

To remove that right, he argued, would be to risk 'anarchy and confusion'. It was, in other words, a form of 'safety valve' which in Dundee as in other Scottish towns released tensions which might otherwise have led to a major explosion. Attempts on the part of the authorities to interfere could end painfully, as Dundee's provost discovered to his cost on Queen Victoria's birthday in 1839 when during what was described by a witness as a 'gae row', his head had been cut. (Afterwards his assailant was confined to prison for 90 days.)

Although the worst excesses of the overwhelmingly young rioters were contained by determined action on the part of Dundee's police force, established under a local Police Act in 1824, it was not until well into the Victorian era that what the *Advertiser* in 1851 called the 'fiery ordeal' became a cooler affair. Only within living memory have the street bonfires which were lit on Victoria Day disappeared.

CHAPTER 10

Social Life in Victorian Dundee

The Swelling City: New Faces

The earlier signs of change in the character of Dundee's social life were simply straws in the wind. The hurricane hit in the later 1820s, 1830s and 1840s. The mushrooming mills and increased numbers of handlooms required workers. Migration into Dundee of course had been taking place from the time of the burgh's foundation. In the eighteenth and early nineteenth centuries the flow became faster in all of Scotland's manufacturing towns, although as has been noted Dundee's rate of growth was nowhere near the fastest. It was still marked though—the population doubled between 1766 and 1801, to just over 26,000 inhabitants. Most came from the adjacent rural areas of Angus and Fife, but Highland migration into Dundee was also substantial enough to support the establishment of a Gaelic chapel in 1791. Nevertheless while there were 809 Highland-born residents of Dundee in 1851, this accounted for no more than just over one per cent of the total population.

In the first two decades of the nineteenth century however growth had slowed. It was the calm before an unprecedented demographic storm. Dundee's population soared thereafter, reaching 45,355 in 1841. It had more than doubled again by 1861, to 90,568. It was only after 1881, as the jute industry's progress began to falter, that the rate moderated, and indeed has never since been over one per cent per annum, often much less. During the decade 1831–41, when the town's population rose by well over one-third, the annual rate of increase was more than four per cent.

Part of the rise can be explained by periodic extensions of the burgh's boundaries, which brought Lochee (1859) and later Broughty Ferry (1913) under Dundee's umbrella. Most however was the result of massive immigration. So great was this that by 1851 only 46 per cent of those living in Dundee had been born there. Until the 1840s most incomers came from the surrounding counties. In the later years of that decade however what since the 1820s had been a steady stream of Irish immigrants became a flood: by 1851 the 14,889 Irish-born residents of Dundee (three times as many as in 1841) accounted for 19 per cent of the town's total population.

Overwhelmingly the newcomers came to find work, in textiles. Large numbers tore up their roots in the counties of Cavan and Monaghan; fewer did the same in Leitrim, Fermanagh and Sligo. Links between Dundee and the north central counties of Ireland had been established through the flax and yarn trade. The availability of cheap passages over the Irish Sea forged them more intimately, as conditions worsened in Ireland and job opportunities expanded in Dundee.

Many of those who came were young, unmarried females, travelling in groups of two or three, although families arrived too, attracted by the range of economic opportunities in configurations with which they had been familiar; the adult male or males could find work in handloom weaving while the female members of the household assisted as winders or entered the spinning mills.

In 1871 some 12 per cent of Dundee's population was still Irish-born, but the influx from Ireland had passed its peak and soon tailed off altogether. Yet immigration into Dundee from overseas did not come to a halt. Trading connections had brought businessmen such as Isaac Weinberg and Daniel Jaffé from Germany in the mid-1800s. Larger numbers, some of whom were also merchants, came from the same country in the 1870s. Push rather than pull factors account for the appearance of Lithuanians after 1881, as a result of the repressive policies of Tsar Alexander III. Jews, forced to flee from Russia, arrived too, as did a steady trickle of Italians, driven abroad owing to population pressure on agricultural holdings in north Italy.

Although both the Germans and the Jews managed to establish themselves in Dundee to the extent that they had their own church and synagogue respectively, the numbers of all non-Irish immigrant groups to Dundee were always small compared to those which settled elsewhere in Scotland. On their way to the USA, it was much more likely that they would end up on the west coast. Thus in 1911 there were only 142 Jews in the city, and some 100 Lithuanians.

There were more Italians, but even in 1921, the peak year, there were only 321, of a Scottish total of 5,150. Apart from Ireland, England was the main non-Scottish source of incomers, their numbers rising steadily from 1841; even so, the proportion of English men and women in Dundee in 1911 was smaller than in Scotland as a whole. Almost certainly this is to be accounted for by the relative absence of professional employment opportunities in Dundee, a subject which will be discussed shortly.

The Fall: The Social Cost of Prosperity

The social consequences of the appearance of the swelling sea of new faces in the early decades of the Victorian era were profound. Plague had disappeared but only to be replaced by other killer diseases—some of which had made an appearance earlier—such as cholera (1832, 1849, 1853 and 1866), typhus (1837 and 1847), smallpox, measles, whooping cough and scarlet fever. Typhus lingered on in Dundee—and occasionally reached minor epidemic proportions—into the 1880s. The spread of these had much to do with chronic overcrowding, notably in the vicinity of the mills and factories: as early as 1841 the Rev George Lewis of St David's parish, which included the Scouringburn and Hawkhill districts, reported that on a recent visit to English industrial towns such as Birmingham and Manchester he had 'looked in vain for the evidence of a deeper physical degradation than I meet daily in Dundee'. Remarkably, only two decades earlier, districts such as Scouringburn and Pleasance had been relatively

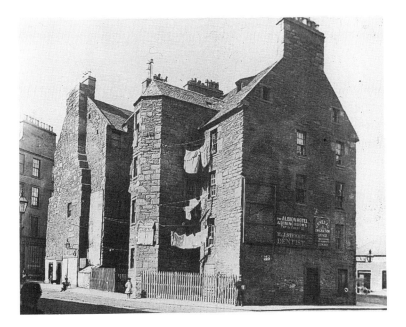

This eighteenth century tenement in Union St was used as a temporary hospital during outbreaks of cholera in Dundee in the 1820s and 1830s. The photograph was taken in the late nineteenth century. *Dundee Art Galleries & Museums.*

View from the rear of the Town House, late nineteenth century. This is a vivid portrayal of the cramped and overcrowded housing conditions which produced some of the highest levels of disease and mortality in Scotland. *Dundee Archive and Record Centre.*

open (Polepark was pasture land). In spite of the encroachment of mills, several nurseries and market gardens were laid out there.

In large part the squalor which so appalled Lewis was associated with cramped living conditions, as property was further and further sub-divided to house the incomers. The existing housing stock however was insufficient to cope with such a massive influx of people. Few employers built houses for their workers. The belated efforts of Malcolm Ogilvie & Co in this regard in the 1890s in Brown Constable St and Dundonald St were exceptional. It was with some reluctance that Baxters had earlier built some houses in Lyon St. One brutal statistic exposes the severity of the problem: while Dundee's population rose by 30,000 between 1841 and 1861, only 568 new houses were built. Living space then was at a premium: in 1911 more than two-thirds of Dundee's population lived in one- and two-roomed dwellings in what were usually three- and four-storey tenement blocks. By this means builders and investors obtained the best returns from the limited space which was available for house construction.

What was built was generally poor: piped water only became widely available in the 1870s. Private bathrooms were rare. Common doorways, stairs and yards were the norm. Privacy was impossible, playspace for children non-existent, except for those living near Magdalen Green—or Guthrie St, Dudhope Place and Blackscroft, where there were small playgrounds. It is hardly surprising that at 20.0 per 1,000 at the turn of the twentieth century Dundee's death rate was amongst the highest in urban Scotland. Only Glasgow was worse. In some districts, such as Meadowside-Murraygate and Scouringburn, the rates were two and three times as high.

Another contributory factor, particularly where cholera was concerned, was the town's pitifully inadequate water supply. As early as 1799 it was said that this would 'disgrace the meanest village in Britain'. Worse was to come, as demand grew. Much was sold in the streets from carts in which it was brought from the town's main wells at Logie Spout (in Milnbank Rd), Smellie's Wynd (off Lochee Rd) and Ladywell (at the foot of Hilltown). Its quality was appalling: an analysis in 1868 of the water from the Ladywell showed that it was 'nothing but a very thoroughly purified sewage'. Nearby was a slaughterhouse. One Board of Health inspector remarked that he had seen in Dundee, 'spectacles so extremely offensive and disgusting that he could scarcely have conceived their existence possible in a civilised country'.

The Dundee Water Act of 1845 produced respectable returns for the shareholders of the private water company which it had authorised—contrary to the wishes of the Town Council—but a highly unsatisfactory supply of water, from Monikie and Stobsmuir. It was not until the local authority took over and appointed as engineer Frederick Bateman, the designer of Glasgow's and Manchester's waterworks, (and a little later, James Leslie, of Edinburgh Waterworks), and initiated three further water acts, in 1871, 1872 and 1874, that significant improvement occurred. It was at this time, with the raising of the water level of the Loch of Lintrathen by 20 feet, and the construction of Clatto Reservoir, that the basis of the present system was laid. At the same time concerted efforts were made to deal with the town's waste water, which was taken to the Tay in some 46 miles of underground sewage pipe.

In other respects too the town's existing facilities were simply incapable of coping with the inrush of people. The 'Old' or King St Infirmary, to which the first patients were admitted in 1798, had by the 1840s become 'utterly inadequate'. Eventually the board of directors decided to move to a new site (to the east of Dudhope castle) on which was to be built the present day Royal Infirmary. Then the largest public building in Dundee and capable of treating 280 patients, it was opened to a grateful public in February 1855. Fever cases however continued to pose massive problems—indeed in 1863 and 1864 no less than three successive medical superintendants and the matron became typhoid victims—although it was not until 1890 that King's Cross fever hospital was opened.

As the population grew, so too did the incidence of petty crime and violent assaults on 'persons of property', and accordingly the number of arrests made by the town's newly-formed police force went up. The result was serious overcrowding in the townhouse gaol, which become so bad by 1834 that even the sheriff-substitute of Forfarshire declared himself shocked by 'what the prisoners have to endure'. In one cell alone, which measured 20 feet by 11, there were 14 male prisoners. Further accommodation which was made available in the Steeple tower had its drawbacks too, not the least of which was that if those incarcerated within it were to have any water, it had to be carried up 87 steps of a spiral staircase.

The opening of a new purpose-built bridewell or prison three years later solved that particular problem however, although the numbers of neglected juveniles who turned from begging to crime to survive posed another: in 1846 no less than 113 children under the age of 14 were committed to Dundee Prison alone. Inspired by Aberdeen's example, in the same year Dundee's first 'school of industry', in Temple Lane, opened its doors—behind which its inmates received food, elementary education and training. Pressure of numbers forced the Dundee Industrial Schools

Not the *Unicorn*, but the training ship *Mars*, home for many generations of Dundee lads until she was broken up in 1929. *Dundee District Libraries Photographic Collection.*

Society to move the school however, first to Ward Rd and in 1878 (in the case of boys) to Baldovan. Girls remained at Ward Rd until the opening of Balgay in 1896. For boys who looked as though they might be slipping down the slope towards delinquency, despite its grim appearance, the best prospects were to be had after a period on board the *Mars* training ship, brought by tug into the Tay in August 1869.

Conflict and Conciliation

As the reference above to crime and punishment suggests, social tensions were growing. One cause was the appearance of and public reaction to the Irish, although all immigrant groups were subject to hostile treatment at some time or another. The intensity of anti-German feeling during the First World War for instance (which was by no means confined to Dundee) persuaded most of Dundee's German community to leave.

Almost a century beforehand there had been a powerful current of anti-Catholic feeling in Dundee, which had been whipped up in 1829 as Parliament moved towards Roman Catholic emancipation. The following year, on 6 June, grumbling hostility between the natives of Dundee and some Irish immigrants, which had at first been channelled into a series of boxing matches on top of the Law, exploded into angry assaults on the Irish. Accused of bringing down wage levels, their assailants, whose 'avowed purpose' was to drive them out of the town, attacked a number of their houses as well as the Catholic chapel in Meadowside.

Not surprisingly, the Irish incomers tended to stick closely together. Although they were to be found in most parts of the town where dwellings could be rented cheaply, analysis of the 1841 Census reveals clusters of Irish households in close proximity; what is also clear is that there was relatively little inter-marriage between the Scots and the Irish, who, wrote one commentator (somewhat exaggeratedly) earlier this century, were 'with us but not of us'. He had failed to recognise that the Irish had to a large degree made Dundee what it was and were an integral part of its unique character: 'us' also included 'them'.

Although dramatic, incidents such as that described above were comparatively rare (that most Irish immigrants were Catholic and Orangeism was weak in Dundee is a partial explanation for this). Yet moves towards integration were delayed by the active role adopted by the Roman Catholic Church in creating an Irish community within the community. Although weakened by internal squabbling the Catholic Church managed to establish a powerful presence in Dundee, in the form of churches such as St Andrews in the Nethergate (1836) and St Clements, Lochee (1860), schools and a variety of distress-relieving parochial services amongst which was the charitable work of the Society of St Vincent de Paul, a Catholic Day Nursery and a Working Mothers' Restaurant.

The Catholic Church was not alone in going out amongst the poor: the Episcopalians reckoned around 1860—after the Hilltown mission church of St Salvador had been founded—that they had a 'flock' of 6,000, 'mainly of the destitute classes'. Although the immediate effect of the Disruption of 1843 was to weaken the Church of Scotland, with six of its 17 congregations seceding to the Free Church, inter-church rivalry led to the building of several new churches (12 and seven respectively between 1850 and 1900), mission-houses and schools in those districts where there were none, with the object of saving souls and instilling sound habits amongst the city's children.

The fact is that such intervention was necessary in Dundee, its massive working class population more vulnerable than any of the others of its size to the fluctuating fortunes of its single dominant industry: 'Almost everybody in Dundee', one observer wrote, 'is interested, more or less, in the fortunes of jute'.

Classes Apart

Dundee's middle class on the other hand was relatively small. In 1861 the percentage of individuals in 'professional' employment was 11.6, compared to the Scottish average of 16.6. The number of people who could be classified in this way was less than half that of similarly-sized Aberdeen. Because Dundee was less of a regional centre, openings in the legal and banking professions were especially scarce. Industrial entrepreneurs, managers and clerks were not. Despite the fortunes which some Dundonian textile magnates amassed however, less than one per cent of the personal estates of the city's deceased in 1881 were worth more than £10,000. The comparable figure for Glasgow was five per cent, for Scotland as a whole, four per cent.

Yet much wealth left Dundee, invested by men from the Baxter, Cox, Gilroy and Grimond dynasties overseas, notably in US railways, sent there through the Scottish-American Trusts launched by Robert Fleming. Born in Liff Rd, Lochee, Fleming first became acquainted with the world of finance when employed as a book-keeper with Edward Baxter & Son. Speculative ventures in land and cattle ranching were initiated by William Lowson, and run by William Reid and William Mackenzie. Oregon and Texas were the favoured states. In the ten years after 1873, the date of the first investment trust, some £5 million (equivalent today to around £200 million) flowed westwards out of Dundee.

A consequence of Dundee's unbalanced occupational structure (allied to lower per capita income levels) was that the adverse effects of the trade cycle, which might otherwise have been countered by the spending power of regularly paid, salaried employees, raged unchecked. Another was that new consumer industries, which might have helped to diversify Dundee's 'dangerously lopsided' economy, were slow to arrive. The situation did improve though, and by 1911 Dundee had gone some way towards catching up with the other Scottish cities, with almost one in five of those in work being in middle-class occupations.

Work and residential patterns were not the same thing however. One of the Rev George Lewis's fears in 1841 was that the arrival of the railway was making it easy for 'capitalists' to live in the country and thereby 'convert Dundee into one great work-shop'. He was right: in the early 1900s it was reckoned that 'half of better class Dundee lives out of Dundee'. Those lower down the social scale had little choice but to live as near as possible to their places of work, at least until the appearance of tramways, the first of which, in 1877, ran along Perth Rd to Blackness Toll. By the end of the century Baxters's workers were being provided with a special early morning service which ran down the hill to Dens Works from the north end of Albert St.

The beginning of the middle-class exodus can be dated (with some precision) to the second half of the 1830s. Previously, a substantial proportion of Dundee's more affluent citizens had lived in flatted properties (and a handful of self-contained houses) in the commercial quarter of the town, Cowgate, Wellgate, Bain Square and Meadow St. Discomfited by pressure on their living space and concerned about the spread of infectious diseases, numbers of them began to leave what had often been mixed residential areas and settle in the cleaner air of Newport, which was easily reached by steam ferry, Newtyle (linked to Dundee by rail in 1831), West Ferry along Douglas Terrace (1838) and into Broughty Ferry, once a fishing village but by the end of the 1800s better-known for its businessmen, lawyers, doctors and churchmen, and with the establishment of University College, professors and lecturers.

Within the town too, a process of physical segregation was taking

BROUGHTY FERRY FROM RERES HILL

Broughty Ferry, one of Dundee's suburbs, where from the 1830s middle- and upper-class Dundonians fled in order to escape from the encroachment of textile mills and factories, immigrant workers, overcrowding and infectious diseases. On the right is Reres Mount, one of the more modest of the palatial residences built by Dundee's jute 'barons'.

place. Pasture land on the lower slopes of the Law was feued for the building of middle-class villas such as those at 1–3 Dudhope Terrace (1840). Not all contemporaries were impressed by the location though: commenting on the 'new Cottages building at the top of Constitution Brae' in 1830, Thomas Handyside Baxter thought that while the view was good the plan as a whole was odd, 'distant from all Markets and in the Winter I would think this an uncomfortable residence'.

He was struck too by the speed at which the ground was being built over in Lochee, where Mary Jobson, later Mrs Home Scott, wife of James Scott, writer in Dundee, had gone with their family for country holidays earlier in the century, with hopes that the hawthorn and laburnum would be in flower so that they could decorate the horse and cart which took them there each year around the fourth of June, King George III's birthday. Few shared Baxter's concerns about amenities however and building went on—around 1851 the spacious detached and semi-detached villas of Laurel Bank, Prospect Place, Constitution and Union Places began to be laid out, screened and secured from the works and inhabitants of the cramped and air-less backlands of Rosebank, to the west of the Hilltown, by a purposely built high stone wall. It was several years later, from the 1870s and into the twentieth century, that most of the mansion houses in the Dudhope district, the west end along and off Perth Rd, and in Broughty Ferry, were designed and constructed.

The new residential patterns confirmed the great gulf between the rich and relatively well-off and the working-class majority in Dundee. For example, the valuations of the Albany Terrace homes of solicitors, merchants and retired bank agents ranged from £38 to £65, compared to the £3–£5 rentals paid by tenters, labourers, porters and the like for their single rooms in some parts of the Hilltown. The grandest and most lavishly decorated houses however were usually those owned by the proprietors of Dundee's textile firms.

In these were held sumptuous eight-course dinner parties and more intimate dances and musical evenings (although both the last two were more refined occasions than their later eighteenth and early nineteenth century counterparts when 'Scotch reels' and other much more energetic dances were in vogue). Rivalry in the 1850s and '60s in particular drove their owners to demand of their architects and designers the latest and most prestigious fashions in building and interior decoration, exemplified in the Gilroys's Gothic palace of Castleroy and the Grimonds's Carbet Castle. Both however were victims of dry rot and had to be demolished. These were at the top of the ladder; far below, but still a rung or two above the tenement were the terraced or semi-detached villas of Maryfield and Downfield.

Women, Men and Children

More than anything else, what marked Victorian Dundee off from the rest of urban Scotland, was that overwhelmingly, it was a 'woman's town'. Nowhere else was there such a high proportion of females: in 1901 there were in Dundee 17,421 more women than men over the age of 20.

Predominantly they worked in textiles: 83 per cent of Dundee's working women were so employed in 1851, a proportion which altered little (it grew slightly) before 1911. Equally remarkable was the way in which married women in Dundee scorned the 'angel in the house' role which Victorian ideology had prescribed for them. Just under a quarter of married women were known to be in more or less permanent paid employment in Dundee, where they were 'artisans, not housekeepers', and highly esteemed too, as they were thought to be more regular workers than their unmarried sisters. The figure for working widows was even higher. In Aberdeen only three per cent of married women worked. One consequence for Dundee, 'a city where men were frequently dependent upon the earnings of mothers, sisters and daughters', was that traditional household roles were reversed. Many men, stripped of the patriarchal power which they could elsewhere assume with their bread-winning function, were reduced to the status of 'kettle-bilers'.

A profoundly tragic statistic is that relating to infant mortality; Dundee's was the highest in Scotland. Although historians still dispute the precise causes of this, there is no doubt that it is linked, one way or another, with the fact that so many women, married and unmarried, worked for abysmally low wages and lived in squalid conditions.

Males had a place in the coarse textile trade, but if they were not overseers, beamers, tenters, weavers, mechanics, joiners, firemen, warehousemen, clerks or labourers, they were likely to be young: in the early 1900s it was reported that around 800 youths under 20 were 'turned adrift'

Handloom weaver and spinner using hand spinning-wheel, Mid-Wynd Works, c.1850. This was towards the end of the hand weaving era. Already power looms, worked by females, had begun to replace male hand weavers. *Dundee Art Galleries & Museums.*

from the mills and factories each year, their usefulness for such work at an end. They would have had to have been paid adult male rates. It was only in the finishing departments where men were in the majority, working as calenderers, lappers (who made up lengths of finished cloth) and packers. Alternative employment was hard to find. Carting was one option, the army another—if they were fit enough. In a survey conducted by the army recruiting office in Dundee during 1904 just over half of the males who presented themselves were turned away, undersized, underfed and under strength. Dundonians—male and female—who worked in the preparing and spinning departments of some jute mills were the 'poorest specimens of humanity' one factory inspector had ever seen.

It was little wonder. Textile wages in Dundee were 20 per cent below those of Glasgow in the 1870s, the nineteenth century peak. Even in 1905 the typical wage in spinning was in the region of 12s. Weavers could earn two, three or four shillings more, but work in both spinning and weaving was irregular and periods of privation were the norm. Nor could they improve things by leaving: wages for females in the dressmaking and millinery trades trades were low too. Worst was hand-sewn jute sacking, the preserve of unknown numbers of the 'the lowest class of workers', who might get 6s. a week for work they slowly carried to squalid homes in bundles weighing half a hundredweight or more from the factory or calendar and then back again. Confectionery and biscuits were said to pay 'wonderfully well' in 1903, but the work was often seasonal. In the textile industry virtually the only people who were paid over £1 per week were male mechanics (who could earn as much as 33s.), overseers, some calender workers and lappers. At the bottom of the ladder were the 'half-timers', the children, who until 1892 could be as young as eight, who combined school attendance with mill and factory work. More than 300 other juveniles delivered milk and sold newspapers.

Though most of Dundee's female mill and factory workers were badly paid they were not meek or passive victims of the industrial system. They necessarily adapted themselves to their broadened responsibilities, became hardened to the remorseless discipline of the steam-driven spinning frame and powerloom, and within the works developed an impenetrable sign language by which they could communicate over the machinery's incessant rattle. Outside they could be coarse; many of them drank to excess and appeared in the police courts on drunk and disorderly charges more often than 'respectable' Victorian women should have; it was not uncommon for them to use snuff, to clear noses clogged with jute dust.

Dundee's women workers however did not form a single undifferen-

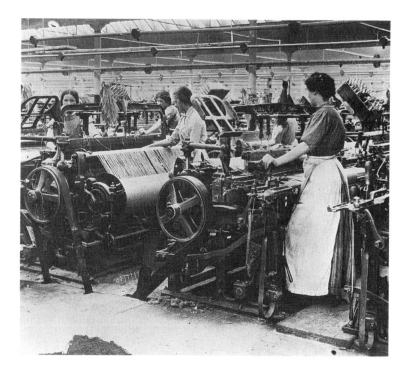

Weaving shed, Dens, *c*.1910. Females on powerlooms had begun to replace male handloom weavers in the 1840s. Although not shown here, overseers and other supervisory posts were still held by males, whose wages were considerably higher than the 12–14s. per week which these weavers would have earned. *University of Dundee Archives*.

tiated mass. Contemporaries associated the most unruly behaviour with the 'low mill' and the spinning flats where flax and jute were prepared; it was here that the unskilled could find a place, along with vagrants and 'the unfortunates whom society disowns', widows and 'the wives of incorrigible loafers'. In their habits, attitudes and dress the millgirls could usually be distinguished from the winders and weavers, who were 'aye that uppish like', according to one ex-spinner. Weaving was certainly a cleaner job. Weavers typically wore a hat and gloves to work, aspired to marry 'a wee bitty better men', and once married, tended to remain at home, priding themselves on their cleaner stairs and 'respectable' status. Even so, a return to work was not out of the question, when their husbands were laid off, or in order to supplement the family income.

Yet distinctions can be too sharply drawn. Weavers and spinners could come from the same family. Not all millgirls were 'of hard voice and rough manners'. Mary Slessor, the missionary, was once a half-timer with Baxters. Nor were weavers altogether absent from street disturbances.

In truth there is a case for focussing attention on the mills and factories individually, as conditions and workplace relations in them were far from uniform. The district from which a millgirl came could make a difference too: the Overgate for example had a particularly bad reputation. In the 'better class' mills, it was reported in the *People's Journal* in 1903, 'the honour of the firm is jealously guarded by the employees', who resented the 'introduction of those who are not likely to do credit to "the wark" '. It is worth noting too that many more prostitutes—and men—were charged with being drunk and disorderly, while for both sexes the crude statistics are unfair as they conceal the number of habitual offenders; one individual apparently appeared before the bench 260 times. Drink and drunkards were easy targets for moralisers. There were however some enlightened contemporaries who recognised that so miserable were living conditions in some districts that the 'inmates' would welcome 'any means of escape' and find the attractions of the public house irresistible.

Oppressed but Not (Quite) Broken

Regardless of occupation, Dundee's women have recently been described as a 'defiant sisterhood'. Rightly so. To the discomfort of their employers and male trade unionists such as the Rev Henry Williamson who favoured more formal—and conciliatory—methods and forms of worker organisation (through his Mill and Factory Operatives Union, formed in 1885), they engaged in spontaneous, often localised, strikes, during which they paraded through the streets, shouting, gesticulating and singing as they marched towards the Cowgate, where the offices of the town's leading merchants and manufacturers were still concentrated, even though they no longer lived in the vicinity. Male authority was mocked within the workplace too, as is recorded in the song *The Spinner's Wedding*. One verse runs:

> The shifters they're a dancin
> The spinners singin tae
> The gaffer's standin watchin
> But there's nothin he can dae.

The readiness of females to challenge was not confined either to the mill and factory or textiles. Fanny Wright was Dundee-born (in 1795), and campaigned ardently for women's rights in North America. In 1871, Dundee's comparatively small army of domestic servants (smaller in part because there were fewer middle-class households), became embroiled in a heated dispute with their mistresses which attracted attention as far afield as London and even San Francisco. Their demands were for fewer hours, more holidays, no Sunday cooking and the right not to wear their 'flag' or cap, which they perceived to be the mark of their 'slavery'.

Women were able to redress the balance in other ways too. Dundee's high illegitimacy rate has been interpreted as a form of demonstration of female independence. Yet almost certainly it owed something to the uneven sex ratio, which gave males considerable leverage as far as physical relations between the sexes was concerned. They had even more if they were mill overseers or mechanics. Judging by the sheriff court records however, the ascendancy of many men was short-lived as more often than under the kirk rule of the previous century they found them-selves brought to heel, the details of their sexual adventuring laid out before the court, and orders made to provide financial support for their offspring until they reached the age of ten.

Responses, Religion and Recreation

Dundee in the great age of jute though should not be portrayed simply as a community at war with itself. In recognition of the potential dangers of class-based conflict inherent in a working and living environment which at its worst had much in common with Charles Dickens's fictional 'Coketown', many of Dundee's business and municipal leaders took steps to ameliorate some of the worst effects of breathtakingly rapid economic expansion and assuage 'popular discontent'. This was entirely prudent, for in the 1830s and early 1840s they had seen just what a potent force collectively organised outrage could be. The threatened Chartist rising threat of 1842 had been particularly frightening, and softened attitudes on both sides of the class divide. Some 755 Special Constables had to be recruited by the Town Council to defend the mills and factories, although the hastily gathered force included 63 pensioners who were hired at 1s. a day for each of the two days they were required.

Accordingly, men such as Sir John Ogilvy, Thomas Neish and Edward Baxter contributed energy and funds towards the establishment of

Opening of Baxter Park in September 1863. Massive crowds turned out on this occasion, in part to show their gratitude to Sir David Baxter, the park's major benefactor. Victorian Dundee was woefully short of space for recreation. *Dundee District Libraries Photographic Collection.*

working men's coffee and reading rooms, model lodging houses, ragged schools, allotments and temperance societies. Baxter Park, opened in 1863 by Earl Russell, the Prime Minister, before an estimated 70,000 crowd, was a spectacular example of employer-led paternalism, this time on the part of Sir David Baxter. 16,731 people were sufficiently moved by his benevolence—and the prospect of breathing fresher air—to contribute to a statue of Sir David, which was placed in the park's pavilion.

Private benefaction was followed by municipal endeavour too, as in the laying out of Magdalen Green as a public park, as a means of providing employment in the early 1840s, and the acquisition of Balgay Hill in 1871. This provided Dundonians with their second altogether new 'place of recreation'.

Other green spaces beyond the cramped streets and backlands which were opened to public access were The Law (1878), Dudhope Park (1893), Lochee Park (1899) and Victoria Park (1906). Nevertheless, portions of fortunes which owed not a little to the toil and sweat of countless working men, women and children continued to trickle back into the civic pool: often this is reflected in the names of places and institutions, such as Caird Hall and Caird Park, which were funded by the textile magnate Sir James Key Caird (1837–1914), of Ashton Jute Works. There are many more examples. Such giving though should not be seen simply (and cynically) as a means of achieving immortality in stone and trees; Caird for instance also provided the wherewithal for the Royal Infirmary's out-patient department as well as a Woman's and a Cancer Hospital, and later, Camperdown House and Park.

Religion provided further relief for many, and a guide to moral behaviour, especially amongst the artisan class—the well-paid males in engineering and shipbuilding—although as has been seen, the various Churches cast their nets widely and deeply through the social ranks. An example of the former is John Sturrock, a millwright at Lilybank Foundry whose diary of the mid-1860s reveals a young man of regular habits, distressed if he lay in bed late, who improved himself by reading poetry, portions of encyclopaedias and mechanics manuals and studying arith-metic, and spent his Sundays walking, often in Baxter Park, visiting, reading pious literature and attending at least one church service.

In this though Sturrock was not typical. Despite the tireless efforts of their adherents, the churches could do little to alter the fact that attendance at Sunday services in working class Dundee was significantly lower than in the nearby suburb of Broughty Ferry, although unlike England but in common with Scotland's other urban conurbations, attendance in Dundee in 1851 was higher than the surrounding rural area.

For those it touched, religion could blunt the edge of opposition to a system which was clearly—and necessarily—exploitative. George Wat-son, the 'Roper Bard', a ropemaker who wrote poetry in his spare time, recognised in his 1885 poem 'Trade and Politics' that his fellow workers' backs 'were at the wa' and 'princes made of jute oppress ye', but his plea was for free education and Christian brotherhood, not revolution. Nor was James Myles, author of *Chapters in the Life of a Dundee Factory Boy*, the critic of industrial capitalism he is sometimes credited with being. The *Factory Boy* is no autobiography but a campaigning novel, a quasi-tem-perance tract and an appeal on behalf of the virtues of self-improvement. Myles, a one-time Chartist and later a bookseller, was an ardent advocate of co-operation between masters and their employees.

Ellen Johnson, a powerloom weaver who had worked in factories in Glasgow and Belfast before coming to Dundee, where she was employed at both Verdant Works and Chapelshade Factory, could write powerful vernacular poetry on behalf of the poor, 'The Last Sark' for example, which rages at injustice and the lack of concern of the better off for the those with no work—'What care some gentry if they're weel though a' the puir wad dee'—yet many of her compositions were awkward and to modern eyes too sweetly sycophantic. Tributes to revered employers and their works, as in 'Most Respectfully Dedicated to Mr James Dorward' which opens with the line, 'Dear Chapelshade Factory! once more I hail thee', fail to convince. Yet the sentiments which her poetry reveals appear to have been widely shared amongst Dundonians of her class.

Culture and Industry

So too was an interest in poetry and literature. Some of this was in the tradition of the 'Literary Chartists' (otherwise known as the 'Dundee Republic of Letters'), men such as James Gow and William Thom, weavers, and James Mitchell, a veteran of the ill-fated Chartist 'March to Forfar', who met weekly to discuss politics and poems.

Although their literary efforts were often (poor) imitations of Burns, provincial in content and tone and overloaded with pathos, it is arguable whether any of them were as eccentric as those of the self-styled 'Poet and Tragedian' William Topaz McGonagall. Better described by a modern critic as a 'lickspittle of Victoriana, an opportunist of doggerel', McGonagall had been born in Edinburgh but came as a boy to Dundee where he worked as a weaver. He left, the victim of abuse, cruel hoaxes and probably his own gullibility, in 1894. Newspapers such as Leng's *People's Journal*, published weekly, tapped and opened further the richer section of this literary seam. It was not simply directed at the working classes, it also encouraged their participation via contributions on a variety of subjects. Within a fortnight of the paper's appearance its first poetry competition was announced. Christmas and New Year story competitions were particularly well-subscribed, and indeed such was the weight of popular literary submissions to the editor, William Latto, a Fife-born weaver and, again (significantly), a former Chartist supporter, that Leng was persuaded to publish a sister-paper, the *People's Friend*, a literary miscellany, in 1869.

In short, 'Juteopolis' had a cultured underbelly. A more obvious example of this was the construction of buildings such as the Albert Institute, 'the grandest Albert memorial outside London', designed by Sir George Gilbert Scott, the leading Victorian architect working in the then fashionable Gothic style. Baxter Park had been laid out with the advice of Sir Joseph Paxton, architect of London's great Crystal Palace. To coincide with the opening of the Albert Institute (in 1867) the British

Some of the 'high girders', from the first Tay Rail Bridge, which collapsed during an exceptionally strong gale on 28 December 1879. Inside the wreckage is the macabre sight of one of coaches of the ill-fated train. *Valentine Collection, University of St Andrews Archives.*

Association for the Advancement of Science was invited to convene in Dundee. In part this was a reflection of a rising civic pride. Another influence was the strong sense of social inferiority of many of Dundee's businessmen; involvement in 'trade' was looked on rather sniffily in established circles and involvement in the art world was one way of demonstrating that they were men of taste. Some genuinely were.

Thus as in other great industrial and commercial centres such as Glasgow, Leeds and Liverpool, Dundee's merchants and manufacturers were major buyers and sponsors of fine art. The Scottish landscape painter William McTaggart and other contemporary artists owed much to the patronage of businessmen such as J C Bell, a flax merchant whose house was in the Cowgate, James Guthrie Orchar and William Robertson, textile engineers, and John Keillor, of the jam and marmalade manufacturing firm which had been established by James Keillor in 1797. Robertson was the first chairman of the Dundee Art Union, founded in 1877 (the present Art Society dates back to 1890); Orchar, who was for a time Provost of Broughty Ferry, was associated with Dundee Art Club and instrumental, with T S Robertson, in establishing a lucrative series of artists' sale exhibitions which were mounted in Dundee between 1877 and 1891. His collection of 302 paintings was bequeathed to the city at his death in 1898, and displayed for several decades (until it closed in 1979) in what became known as the Orchar Gallery in Broughty Ferry. The foundation of Duncan of Jordanstone College of Art, in 1892, was further confirmation of Dundee's commitment to and interest in the visual arts.

These however were largely the concerns of the privileged minority. William Robertson's hopes that the working classes would subscribe to the Art Union were largely disappointed. For one thing the annual subscription of 10s.6d was impossibly high.

Popular leisure pursuits were cheaper, and often more boisterous. Cock-fighting had long gone by the end of the nineteenth century, but cricket was played on Magdalen Green. As in former times, travelling shows and circuses, as well as the town's fairs, continued to attract large crowds. So too did the theatres and music halls: the grandest was Her Majesty's Theatre and Opera House, opened in 1885 in the Seagate, with seats for 1,600 people. (Largely rebuilt after a fire in 1941, this is now the Cannon cinema.) Shortly after their first appearance in Dundee in 1895, 'moving pictures' could be seen both at fairs and in the music halls. Football was growing in popularity as a spectator sport at locations such as West Craigie Park, the original home of Dundee FC (formerly 'Our Boys' club, formed in 1877). Dens Park was opened in 1899. Although the city could boast a number of clubs, some disquiet was expressed about the relatively small numbers of males who actually played the game.

Attendance at some of these events could be expensive: no entry fees were required for one of the most common recreations—'promenading' and 'ha'en a gossip'. Saturday night was when cares were cast to the wind. Sundays could be noisy too, especially in Reform St, where young men and women were said in 1876 to have been in the habit of 'perambulating' up and down the street, laughing and engaging in 'loud talking, whistling and unrestrained freedom'. On the other evenings the streets usually quietened after nine. Shopping could still be done until then—later on Saturdays, when the shops remained open to catch the trade which came their way after the public houses closed. For shop assistants though, mainly young unmarried females, this meant long hours—longer than in the mills—90 per week if they worked for licensed grocers.

That Dundee was a 'place for work not for pleasure', can be seen from the numbers who departed—temporarily—on day trips. Fewer had the time off for or could afford longer breaks. The formation of cycling clubs,

Hand barrow used by the police in Dundee to transport drunks to the cells. The humour of the cartoon contrasts with the reality of widespread drunkenness in Victoria Dundee, where a high proportion of those charged were females.

in Broughty Ferry in 1880 and Dundee in 1881, underlines the growing popularity of Sunday cycle runs into Perthshire and Fife. The exodus was greatest during the Dundee holiday. By the turn of the twentieth century some 136,000 people, four out of five of the city's inhabitants, were going on some sort of excursion. A few hundred went by steamer, to Newburgh, Perth, Leith and even Newcastle. Pleasure trips from Dundee had been available from around 1839. The ferry to Newport provided another escape route. Thousands however went by rail.

The first railway track out of Dundee had led to Newtyle (remarkably, as commercial logic pointed to Forfar). Although passenger fares had been low, it was the opening of the Dundee and Arbroath railway in 1838 that heralded a new era for recreational travel, although as has been seen, it also made suburban living practicable for the middle-classes. Broughty Ferry and Monifieth were always popular destinations, but as the rail network extended—the route south opened up with the construction by the North British Railway Company of the first, ill-fated Tay Rail Bridge in 1878—so too did the ambitions of Dundee's travelling public, who were carried on 'Specials' as far away as Edinburgh, Aberdeen and Glasgow. If comparatively few of their fellow-Scots visited Dundee, at least Dundonians were seeing the rest of Scotland. Until 1959 they could depart from any one of three stations, Taybridge and Dundee West (in South Union St), and Dundee East (Dock St).

CHAPTER 11

Government and Politics

Dundee and the Jacobites

Dundee in the seventeenth century had twice been the victim of the national political upheavals of the day, and the ravages of the Civil War came close to destroying the town beyond its capacity to recover. Nor of course did the restoration of the monarchy in 1660, nor the 'Glorious' Revolution of 1689, end the city's involvement in revolutionary politics. Indeed the ousting of James VIII and II began the long and ultimately fruitless struggle to restore the Stewart line to its rightful throne, casting most of Scotland, willing or not, into the turmoil of the '15 and the '45.

Dundee's responses to the Jacobite calls to arms were similar to those of other Lowland towns, though for her own particular reasons. In the immediate aftermath of the 1689 Revolution, the town's rulers had to contend with the threat from her own Constable, Graham of Claverhouse or 'Bonnie Dundee', who, despite having earlier saved the life of William of Orange at the Battle of St Neffe, now stood by his oath of allegiance to James. Rebelling against William and Mary, Claverhouse led a small band of loyal Highlanders against the forces of the Crown, only to be killed at Killiecrankie as his men charged to victory.

James and Claverhouse, however, had been unpopular in Dundee. For generations there had been friction between the town's civic leaders and their hereditary Constable—friction intensified by James's ill-considered decision to force Claverhouse on the town as its Provost. Yet by 1715 the picture had changed. Over the years the Town Council had become increasingly sympathetic to the Stewarts, for reasons felt widely through-out Scotland—dissatisfaction with the Union of 1707, and the poor state of the economy. In 1714 they took care to welcome the Hanoverians and agreed to celebrate the accession of George I, but in the following year, when the Old Pretender appeared at the head of a band of 300 men, he was proclaimed at the Cross with general approval and the support of the powerful Town Clerk, Alexander Wedderburn.

In 1745 there was another change of heart, as the Town Council now

John Graham of Claverhouse—'Bonnie Dundee'—remained loyal to the Stuarts after William of Orange was proclaimed King in 1689. Claverhouse perished on the battlefield of Killiecrankie, where his rebel army won a remarkable victory over the forces of the King. *Dundee Art Galleries and Museums.*

included the heirs of the Hanoverian supporters elected since 1716. Yet even now when the Jacobites appeared they put up no resistance, explaining apologetically to the King in 1746 that

'We did not give credit to the first accounts brought us of the beginning of the rebellion, but continued unprovided for resistance, till of a sudden we were overcome by a superior force'.

There was little else they could have done. The town was totally without defences, and the town's civic leaders must have been conscious of their being surrounded in the country by landed gentry with Jacobite sympathies, like the Fotheringhams, Sir John Wedderburn of Blackness, and the Earl of Airlie and his son, Lord David Ogilvie. Nevertheless in September 1745 the Council held elections and swore allegiance to George II, despite the presence in the city of a small band of Highlanders, and the installation of David Fotheringham as Governor. Indeed on the King's birthday in October there was a public celebration, and the Jacobite Governor was run out of town. Although he subsequently returned, by mid January the crisis was over, and the last of the rebels had left.

Dundee had in fact suffered little from the brief Jacobite occupation. While in power the rebels had laid and collected taxes, but had been scrupulous in giving receipts and paying for supplies. Little physical damage was caused, though church services were disrupted. In December 1745 the Kirk Session cautiously decided not to issue the royal proclamation for a fast to be held on the 18th, on the ground that 'the town was garrisoned by rebel clans most savage and cruel'.

The 'Radical Toun'

During the '45 the great majority of Dundonians of all classes, it would appear, remained loyal to the ruling dynasty. Few joined the Jacobite army, and of those who did support the cause, few were men of any influence, wealth, or importance. Towards the end of the century, however, Dundee had begun to acquire a more turbulent and radical reputation. Inspired by the writings of Tom Paine and the example of the French Revolution, sharing in the widespread demand in Scotland for burgh reform, but aggrieved also by the high price and scarcity of meal, Dundonians pursued the objectives of reform and the redress of grievances in a variety of ways.

In Dundee as in many other Scottish towns, the outbreak of the French Revolution, the fall of the Bastille, and the early successes of the French Revolutionary Army were celebrated with enthusiasm. In 1790 the Whig Club of Dundee voted an address to the French National Assembly which offered

> 'Our sincere congratulations on the recovery of your ancient and free constitution, and our warmest wishes that liberty may be permanently established in France'

… together with

'our hopes that your example will be universally followed, and that the flame you have kindled will consume the remains of despotism and bigotry in Europe.'

Lest this message be misconstrued, the address went on to laud

'Our Sovereign, the guardian of our constitution and the father of his people, ... and our nobility and clergy who form useful and illustrious members of a state where all are subject to the laws.'

In July a meeting of the more radical Revolution Society pledged the rights of man, the equal representation of the people, the speedy abolition of the slave trade, and the abolition of all religious tests for civil office.

Different societies evidently catered for different degrees of radicalism, from the relatively conservative Whig Club (whose Address nevertheless attracted the condemnation of Edmund Burke in his *Reflections on the French Revolution*) and the Society of the Friends of the People, to the Revolution Society, the Friends of Liberty, and later the Society of United Scotsmen. Two of Dundee's leading radicals, Thomas Fysche

George Mealmaker, a Dundee weaver and leader of the United Scotsmen, was sentenced to fourteen years in a penal colony in 1798 for writing a radical political pamphlet, and died there in 1808.

Palmer, a Unitarian minister convicted of publishing an inflammatory pamphlet in 1793, and George Mealmaker, leader of the United Scotsmen and the author of the pamphlet, were sentenced to transportation to Botany Bay.

The most serious disturbances to occur in Dundee at this time were only partially connected with the campaign for political reform, but arose also out of grievances with the operation of the Corn Laws. On November 16, 1792, a few people gathered in the High Street to celebrate the French Army's 'liberation' of Brussells and tried to plant a Tree of Liberty—a common symbol of the principles of the French Revolution. The tree was soon pulled down by some 'young gentlemen', but on the following Monday an angry mob threatened forcibly to unload a cargo of meal from a ship in the harbour which the customs men refused to release. On the Tuesday a crowd of several hundred paraded through the streets led by a man with a flaming tar barrel on his head and proceeded to attack the houses of a Mr. Webster, the father of one of the 'young gentlemen', and of Lt Fyffe, who had publicly slighted Thomas Palmer. The mob then proceeded to the Town Hall where they insisted upon ringing the bells until persuaded to desist by Provost Riddoch, with the promise that he would seek authority to have the ship unloaded. The crowd moved on the High Street where they built a huge bonfire and set up another Tree, decorated with candles and apples, and bearing a scroll proclaiming 'Liberty, Equality and No Sinecures'.

The motives behind these incidents were clearly mixed. The timing of the first attempt to plant the Tree, the Tree itself, the attacks on the houses of Webster and Fyffe, all suggest that the disturbances were in some way politically inspired. At least two contemporaries, however, Superintendent of Excise James Mitchell and the MP for Forfar, George Dempster, emphasised the customs issue. According to Dempster,

> 'There is a very absurd law, passed the last session, restraining the free commerce in corn between the different parts of this island when prices are at a certain height in London.... One of the causes of discontent at Dundee was the impossibility of landing for sale a cargo of oatmeal from Berwick ... There never was so odd a law.'

Provost Riddoch and his Enemies

Much of the credit for defusing the situation described above must go to the wily, long serving and paternalistic Provost of Dundee, Andrew

Riddoch. Yet Riddoch himself, and the Town Council which he dominated for more than 30 years, were to be in their turn the objects of
criticism and demands for reform.

Riddoch was first elected to the post of Treasurer in 1776, became
Provost in 1787, and continued either to hold or to control that office until
1819. Perhaps inevitably, after so long a reign, his last years were marked
by controversy, and he was accused of corruption and incompetence. But
Riddoch could hardly be held responsible for a system of municipal
government which had operated according to much the same rules for
more than three centuries, and which was little different from that existing
in other Scottish burghs. Nor does there seem to be much substance in the
charges of personal corruption. The attacks on Riddoch are best understood in terms of the determination of the merchant body to have more
say in the running of the town, and also perhaps in terms of the personal
antagonism of Riddoch's business rivals.

The Government of the Town

The form and workings of Dundee's municipal government at the end of
the eighteenth century were much the same as those of the other Scottish
burghs whose constitutions derived from an Act of the Scottish Parliament
of 1469. Under this Act the government of Dundee was placed in the hands
of a Town Council consisting of 20 councillors, made up of the Provost and
four Baillies or magistrates, the Treasurer, the Dean of Guild, and representatives of the Guildry and the Incorporated Trades. Elections were held
annually, but continuity was assured by the rule that, except for the Treasurer, all the officers must already be councillors, and the Provost must
already have been a baillie. 'It must be evident', complained the author of
the essay on Dundee in the *Statistical Account* for 1792, the Rev Small, 'that
the formation of the new council is almost entirely in the hands of their
predecessors', that it was a self-perpetuating and unrepresentative body—'a
fraternity distinct from the community.' 'No appeal', Small claimed with
some exaggeration, 'is made to the Guildry, or to the great body of
merchants who may be considered to be the aristocracy of the place.'

One tactic adopted by Riddoch's opponents then was to try to revive
the powers and position of the Guildry—the ancient association of merchants which, two centuries earlier, had enjoyed very considerable influence in municipal affairs. Initially formed to protect the interests of the
merchants against their competitors from rival burghs, by the early

sixteenth century the Guildry had acquired control over many aspects of burgh administration, including the regulation of weights and measures and the physical development of the town. The Town Council was bound to take their advice on such matters as the level of local taxation, and the uses to which the revenue should be put. By the end of the century, however, effective power over the appointment of the Dean of Guild had passed to the Town Council, and with it the management of the Guildry funds. The explanation for this apparent transfer of authority may perhaps be that in the sixteenth century the power of the merchant class was such that they already controlled the Council, and were merely consolidating their position. Later on, however, as the merchants' wealth and power became eroded by civil war and economic decline, they were unable to wrest back from the Council privileges which they had once willingly surrendered. What is abundantly clear is that Andrew Riddoch had no hand in a process which had taken place many years before.

By the later years of the eighteenth century, Dundee's trade was experiencing something of a revival and the merchant class was consequently gaining in self confidence. There was heavy demand for Dundee's coarse textiles—sailcloth for the Navy, sacking for the sugar plantations of the West Indies, ropes, tarpaulins and other naval supplies. Prosperity for the merchants brought with it a rise in social standing and an influx of new men from outside the burgh anxious to share in the profits of trade. To do so they sought entry to the privileges of burgess-ship, and the period saw some increase in the percentage of burgesses who had acquired their position by purchase rather than through family connections. But the latter remained the predominant route to the ranks of the burgesses, with the old established families defending their position with vigour against such interlopers as Riddoch himself—a native of Comrie. Material success was not of itself the key to social acceptance, and the fact that he was an outsider and a *nouveau riche* sharpened the attack against him. But there were also fellow outsiders to be found amongst Riddoch's opponents, whose motives were just as self-interested as those of the older established merchants. Both groups were concerned to portray themselves as the protagonists of burgh reform against the allegedly corrupt and reactionary Provost. Battle was joined over a number of local issues and *causes celebres*.

The first of these in which the line was clearly drawn between the older families and the new was the fight over proposals to set up a new linen stamping office in the West Port. All linens for export were required to bear a stamp showing that they were of recognised quality, and the stamping office had long been located in the Cowgate, convenient for the old established linen merchants of the area. Over the years, however, linen manufacturing had been spreading into the west end of the town around Hawkhill, and in 1787 Riddoch, who had interests in some of these concerns, petitioned the Board of Trustees in Edinburgh in the name of the Town Council for an additional stamping office. Thus began a long running battle between Riddoch and the Cowgate merchants in which the latter took advantage of the current mood for burgh and parliamentary reform, depicting the Provost as a reactionary barrier to progress and the Town Council as the last bastion of unrepresentative privilege.

In fact the commitment of the merchants to the cause of reform seems to have been both short-lived and, as in the case of the dispute over the stamp office, self serving. As the new century approached and it became increasingly dangerous to be seen to flirt with radicalism, so Riddoch's opponents found a new stick to beat him with—the issue of law and order. For all his apparent success in personally quietening the disturbances of November 1792, Riddoch was criticised for taking too easy going a stance on public disorders. Much more damaging however were accusations of financial corruption—that Riddoch had used his position as Treasurer and then Provost to make profits for himself out of money voted for public works projects.

The Harbour Dispute

For much of his career in city government, Riddoch had been involved in helping to bring about the physical changes required to meet the city's changed economic circumstances. He had been largely responsible for a programme of street widening, as heavy carts replaced pack horses as the principal form of commercial transport. As Treasurer, he had carried out the necessary purchases of land and property preparatory to the construction of Crighton St, and it was while he was Provost that Castle St was constructed and the Council embarked on a plan, which itself aroused some opposition, to widen the Nethergate. But the most controversial of the town's plans for improvement was that for a new harbour. Riddoch was well aware of the need to improve harbour facilities to accommodate the growth in trade, but for the most part dealt with it piecemeal, making improvements and repairs to the existing facilities rather than embarking on major works which would have been beyond the city's financial means. But in 1810 the Town Council published its plans for a new harbour, and immediately found itself at the centre of a storm of criticism.

Part of that criticism was based upon a genuine belief that the Council's plans were inadequate for the long term needs of the town. Others opposed it because it would involve the imposition of a special rate to raise the necessary funds, aware that in previous years only a fraction of the sum raised by harbour dues had been applied directly to the harbour. It was widely believed that some of this money had found itself into Riddoch's pocket, and that with his substantial property interests along the shore he would be bound to profit from the new scheme. A further criticism of the Bill was that it provided for the setting up of a Board of Trustees for the harbour over which the Council would exercise virtually complete control. Opposition to this and subsequent Council schemes for harbour improvements brought together a powerful coalition of Riddoch's business rivals and those who were campaigning for the reform of city government. Chief amongst the latter were the town's leading radicals, George Kinloch, later to be Dundee's first MP, and the reforming editor of the *Advertiser*, Robert Rintoul.

The further details of the harbour dispute need not concern us. What is important, however, is to note that when the Harbour Act finally came to be passed in 1815 it provided for the nomination to the Harbour Commission of representatives of the Guildry. At this time, of course, the Guildry and its Dean were firmly under the control of the Council, and Rintoul, aided by James Saunders, another leading anti-Riddochite, embarked upon a public campaign to revive the powers of the association and restore its independence. It was slow work. Initially the Guildry won the right to inspect the books of the burgh on matters relating to their association, and ultimately, in 1819, the right to elect its own Dean. This victory, however, was less the result of the local campaign than of a general move amongst the Scottish burghs, which had brought about the appointment of a House of Commons select committee to investigate various complaints. The report of that Committee, for all that it endorsed the cause of municipal reform, cannot have satisfied Rintoul and his associates. Dundee, it concluded, was by no means unusual amongst the Scottish burghs in being governed by a self-appointed and unrepresentative oligarchy. It also refused to uphold accusations of malpractice brought against Riddoch and other Council members. Nevertheless, the campaign for reform of the burgh constitution continued under the leadership of Alexander Kay, a spirit merchant, and in 1830 the functions of the Town Council were suspended. An Order in Council in 1831 provided for the election of a corporation by burgesses who had paid burgh rate, pending an Act of Parliament providing for the annual election of one third of the councillors. This special act was superseded in 1833 by the general Burgh Reform Act.

Dundee and Parliamentary Reform

The same year which witnessed the amendment to Dundee's constitution, the report of the select committee on municipal government in the Scottish burghs, and Riddoch's retirement from public office, also saw events which brought Dundee on to the national political stage, and which were to have uncomfortable repercussions for the reform leaders, Kinloch, Rintoul, and Saunders. While recent political activity in Dundee appeared to have centred exclusively upon the concerns of the more or less wealthy and privileged groups, the town could hardly have remained untouched by the larger political debate now being carried on in many of the industrial centres of the country—a debate which often had more to do with the interests of the poor, the underprivileged, and the voteless. Political protest meetings had become more frequent and had attracted huge crowds, persuading the authorities that revolution threatened and must be put down. Of the many disgraceful episodes which resulted, the most deplorable must have been the 'Peterloo Massacre' when, on 16 August 1819, the magistrates of Manchester ordered troops to disperse a large but peaceable crowd gathered to hear a speech by the radical Henry 'Orator' Hunt.

Not very surprisingly, perhaps, the effect of the massacre was to increase rather than diminish popular unrest. In Scotland, well attended protest meetings were held in Paisley and Glasgow, and in Dundee on 16 November a large but orderly crowd gathered on Magdalen Yard Green to be addressed by 'the radical laird' George Kinloch. In his speech to the assembled throng, Kinloch emphasised the need for reform of parliamentary representation, and spoke of the burdens under which the poor of the country had been placed by an unrepresentative government—unnecessary and expensive wars, and excessive taxation. None of these evils would have come about, he was convinced, if the people had been properly represented, and he expressed himself to be 'decidedly an advocate for "Radical Reform" ', on the base of first Annual Elections, secondly Universal Suffrage, and thirdly Political Voting by Ballot.'

Even for its day, the speech can hardly be described as an incitement to revolution, and Kinloch took care to disassociate himself from any such intent. 'We want no Revolution', he declared, 'on the contrary, we want a Reform to prevent a Revolution.' But the speech did contain a sharp

Dundee's first MP, George Kinloch had earlier been forced to flee the country to avoid arrest for alleged sedition. Elected to Parliament in 1833, he died only weeks after taking up his seat. *Dundee Art Galleries and Museums.*

attack on the Manchester magistrates, and a clear implication that the Peterloo affair had been premeditated by the authorities. The 21 Resolutions put to the meeting after the speech included one which explicitly charged the Home Secretary, Lord Sidmouth, with high treason. As a result, Kinloch himself was later charged with sedition, and to avoid certain conviction and punishment he fled to France where he remained until pardoned in 1823.

The Dundee Political Union

The Kinloch affair was followed by something of a lull in Dundee politics, and it was not until 1830 that public meetings again came to be held in support of Parliamentary Reform. At one such meeting in December, resolutions were passed calling for an extension of the franchise, the secret ballot, and for Dundee to have its own Member of Parliament. A petition to this effect contained some 6,400 signatures, which number, commented the *Advertiser*, 'must comprehend nearly the whole of the male population capable of forming an opinion upon a political question.' In February 1831 the Dundee Political Union was formed, with the object of 'obtaining constitutionally an immediate and thorough reform of the House of Commons', and in March premature celebrations were held to mark the passage of the Reform Bill through the Commons, ending in clashes with the police. A further well attended meeting was held on Magdalen Yard Green in 1832 to protest against the resignation of Earl Grey.

But once the proposals for the 1832 Reform Bill had been published, the leaders of the DPU appeared willing to settle for half a loaf. George Kinloch, by now a prominent member of the Union's Council, himself addressed a meeting of the Political Union, in a 'hall completely filled, chiefly by the operative classes,' and advised his audience that

> 'It is true indeed that universal suffrage is awanting, and so are annual Parliaments and vote by ballot, but in the meantime we must take what can be given us.'

When candidates were required to fill Dundee's new seat in the Commons, Kinloch was for many the obvious choice, and he was duly elected. Arriving in London in early February to take his seat, he fell ill of a fever, and died on 28 March 1833.

An important characteristic of the movement for Parliamentary reform in Dundee, as elsewhere, was the degree of collaboration, however temporary, existing between middle and working class activists—what has been called the 'Radical Alliance'. Nowhere was this more evident than within the DPU itself, which may have begun by being dominated by a middle class leadership, (its first chairman was a banker, William Christie) but within which working class radicals soon became influential. This relationship between the classes has, however, been accurately described as 'an unstable collaboration', and the political and economic tensions of the 1830s and 1840s served to drive a wedge between them.

Something of these class differences was reflected in the uncertain path taken by the DPU in the years following the Great Reform Act. The Union debated the question whether it should now dissolve, but decided that there was still work for it to do. It should continue to monitor the effects of the Act, and if necessary press for improvements. It should persist with its plans to disseminate political information within the working class, by the provision of a reading room and library, and it should continue to serve as the only available outlet for working class opinion in the city. For the next few years the Union was active in a number of areas—factory reform, Church affairs, penal reform, and in particular agitation for the repeal of the Corn Laws, to which end it organised a petition. In 1834 a meeting of the DPU passed a number of resolutions in support of Parliamentary reform—extension of the franchise, the equal distribution of Parliamentary seats, payment of MPs and shorter Parliaments.

Dundee Chartism

Two local issues, however, were ultimately to destroy the cohesion of the DPU—serious trade union disputes in 1833/4, and the so-called 'Water War', which dragged on into the 1840s. At issue here was the question whether responsibility for providing badly needed new water supplies should be given to a privately owned joint stock company, or whether there should be a system of assessment on all householders, operated by a publicly owned Water Commission. (Plus ça change ...) One consequence was that the DPU dissolved, to re-emerge in 1836 as the Dundee Radical Reform Association, an organisation which from the first was more clearly identified with the working class—its chairman, James Saunders, was a weaver—and with the Chartist movement. A key event in the political history of Dundee was the visit in 1838 of a delegation from the Birmingham Political Union, a visit which resulted in the recreation of the Dundee Political Union in the same year. With another weaver, James Sanks, as its chairman, the new DPU adopted as its objectives most of the points of the Charter: universal suffrage, annual Parliaments, vote by ballot, equal representation and pay-ment of MPs, though it still retained amongst its aims the repeal of the Corn Laws. Indeed there was no fundamental incompatibility between demands for electoral reform and for repeal of the corn laws, which were represented by Chartist supporters as prime examples of class legislation. At a public meeting held on Magdalen Yard Green in November 1838, the banner carried by employees of Baxter Brothers read 'No corn laws, universal suffrage, vote by ballot'.

Yet tension between middle- and working-class supporters of reform, between anti-Corn Law Leaguers and Chartists, was growing. The former tended to see in repeal a sufficient answer to the major social problems of the day, while the latter saw it as incidental to the larger programme of political reform. And while the DPU and the majority of smaller Chartist organisations in the city, of which by 1840 there were many, favoured a non-violent approach to the achievement of their aims, the middle class was becoming increasingly uneasy. This uneasiness derived in part from the growing popularity of O'Connor, the Chartist agitator, though admittedly his support was much stronger in England than in Scotland. But there was a growing incidence of attempts by radical Chartists to disrupt public meetings called in support of Corn Law repeal. One of these encroachments inspired a deservedly little known poem entitled *Corn Law Agitation and the Chartists* (1839), part of which reads:

> A meeting of a certain class alone
> Those mad fanatics, Chartists, loudly call'd
> They'd have admission be it right or wrong
> They wanted in—the doors on them were shut …
> And if they get not in, to mad excess
> Long sticks and stones and heavy planks they use.

In actual fact there is little evidence to substantiate this picture of Chartist violence, though it was not unusual for opponents of the Corn Laws to try to enhance their own reputation for respectability and political orthodoxy by portraying the Chartists as irresponsible and impractical hotheads. At the same time it was in the interest of Anti-Corn Law Leaguers to support calls for Parliamentary reform, if only as a tactic to attract working class support for their own cause. At an Anti-Corn Law meeting held in the Caledonian Hall in February 1842, where there was a strong Chartist presence, the President of the Dundee Anti-Corn Law Association, Edward Baxter, announced to cheers from the audience that

> 'He had seen the evil of class legislation—his opinions had undergone a change—and he was ready to move forward for an extension of the suffrage.'

Yet later in the same meeting he declared that 'The Corn Law question was ripe for decision, but the other [the suffrage] was not', and successfully urged the meeting to separate the two issues and go at once for repeal. On other occasions, notably at a public meeting on the Green on 4 March, more purely Chartist sentiments won the day, when a resolution for the People's Charter moved by George Duncan, the 'Chartist preacher', was overwhelmingly carried.

By the early 1840s then there still existed a precarious working alliance between middle- and working-class reformers, Anti-Corn Law Leaguers and Chartists, who could see tactical advantage to be gained from maintaining the association, even if they differed radically in terms of priorities. Support for the Charter amongst Dundee's working classes was widespread and articulate. It was not necessarily united. There were many different and separate groups subscribing to Chartist objectives, of which the majority were opposed to 'physical Chartism', and sought to achieve their objectives by meetings and resolutions, rather than by violence and strikes. This moderate position became, however, increasingly difficult to sustain, especially in the context of the worsening economic situation which overtook the city at the beginning of the decade.

Depression Years

In the later 1830s the signs of depression in the town were there for all to see. At the heart of the problem lay the downturn in demand for linen, reflected in a drop in the importation of flax into Dundee from 30,643 tons in 1836 to 21,217 in 1838. The situation worsened steadily in the next year or two, reaching its nadir in 1842. Demand for Dundee's products from its overseas customers appears to have dried up almost completely. In April the *Advertiser* reported that

> 'Accounts from America received a few days ago are worse than ever; the demand for goods of all kinds appears to have totally ceased, and the letters hold out no prospect of any revival'.

By August the same newspaper noted that since the beginning of June, not one cargo had left the harbour for France. The inevitable consequences were a drop in wages, and a sharp rise in unemployment. Edward Baxter himself, in a speech to an Anti-Corn Law meeting in January, was quite explicit about the effects of the recession on the mill workers. 'The statistical returns', he informed his audience,

> 'will show since 1836, weavers wages had been reduced about 25%, employment has been diminished and the people are suffering from dear food.'

The total number of persons employed full-time in factory weaving, he noted, had now been overtaken by the number of those out of work. The public response to this situation on the part of the Baxter brothers and other influential members of Dundee society was typical of the paternalistic approach to poverty in the early Victorian age—they formed a Committee to raise money for the relief of the unemployed.

From the point of view of those thrown out of work, neither Corn Law repeal nor *ad hoc* charity seemed to offer a lasting solution to their plight. On 20 May a march of jobless workmen took place in the city in which the banners carried by the marchers made a direct connection between their demand for relief and their support for the Charter. On one such flag were inscribed the words: 'We are hungry, give us bread or labour that we may feed ourselves by our own industry', while another declared more succinctly: 'The Charter and Nothing Less!' In August a public meeting was held to

> 'consider the present alarming state of the country and to devise means for raising the standard of wages to what it was in 1839'.

The conclusion of the meeting was that the only means of achieving this objective was the Charter. When a poll was carried out to test the town's textile workers' support for strike action, it revealed a general willingness to support a strike if it were political, for the Charter, but not simply for wages. Two dramatic events then ensued: the strike of 23 August, followed by the March to Forfar.

The March to Forfar

Varying reports exist of both these events, but it would seem that they began with a meeting of about 4,000 people on Magdalen Yard Green addressed by local Chartist leaders who urged those present to form a procession to march round the town and persuade the workers in the mills to join in a strike. This plan was followed, and according to one account:

> 'Several of the factories turned out hands to join the movement; and when the procession had reached Hunter Street, near the bottom of Hawkhill, they formed a dense mass covering the whole of Hawkhill to the westward … '

Ignoring the reading of the Riot Act by Sheriff Henderson, the mob proceeded on its way round the mills, from which some workers joined the procession, though many refused to do so. Arriving at Fairmuir, the much depleted assembly agreed a plan to march to Forfar, from where they would call upon local farmers to give them assistance.

In his account of the March, James Myles deliberately parodies the event, which he portrays as a kind of comic military operation. In fact it was probably more pathetic than comic, as the weary marchers, reduced in number from perhaps 400 to no more than two, tired and hungry, arrived in Forfar at about three or four o'clock in the morning. The accounts of their reception differ widely, from that of the enthusiastic pro-Chartist *Dundee Herald* to the dismissive account of the Tory *Courier*, but the latter contains the ring of truth:

> 'The alarm occasioned by the rumoured advance of a large body of rioters from Dundee was great, but when the jaded worn-out Chartists arrived, the feeling was turned to pity. Their brother Chartists refused to turn out in any numbers to their assistance, and their hopes were thus disappointed.'

In the short term, the only tangible result of the March was a number of prosecutions, of the leaders and others, mostly on charges of theft of food—turnips and potatoes—from the fields along the way. In Dundee support for the strike had been only half hearted, and the same was true for Scotland as a whole. The Chartist experience in Dundee produced little or nothing in the way of immediate gains but perhaps more in terms of a legacy for the future—an essential contribution to the political education of the city's working class.

The Liberal Ascendancy

The fruits of that legacy, in the form of a Labour Member of Parliament, were not to be harvested until the next century. From 1832 until 1906, Dundee's parliamentary representation was overwhelmingly Liberal. The premature death of George Kinloch in 1833 obliged the constituency to begin the search for a candidate all over again. Effective power to select a candidate lay in the hands of a junta composed of the more active councillors and the leaders of the DPU, and their choice now fell on the Irish baronet, Sir Henry Parnell. Lacking, of course, Kinloch's close association with local politics, Parnell was nevertheless a candidate likely to command wide appeal amongst the Dundee electorate. With 30 years of parliamentary experience behind him, he was known as a financial expert whose views on economy and fiscal reform commended themselves to the more cautious Liberals, while his opposition to coercion in Ireland attracted the support of the radicals. He was elected unopposed in April 1833, again in the General Election of 1835, and yet again in 1836 when he joined Lord Melbourne's administration. The only threat to his position came in 1837, when Radical dissatisfaction with his attitude in the great water rate controversy (he had sided with the Council) led to the withdrawal of their support in his contest with the Tory candidate John Gladstone (the brother of W E) Even so, he still polled almost twice as many votes as his opponent.

Shortly before the general election of 1841 Parnell was raised to the peerage, and a successor had once more to be found. The local contender was George Duncan, a retired silk merchant, who had aroused controversy by his lack of firmness as an *ex officio* police judge and by his leadership of the assessment faction on the Council. Anxious to find an alternative, the Provost called a meeting of the electors who appointed a committee to look for a more acceptable candidate. Dominated by the Baxters and other leading opponents of the Corn Laws, the committee put forward the name of John B Smith, chairman of the Manchester Chamber of Commerce and Anti-Corn Law Association. But neither of these men were acceptable to the local Chartists, and at the hustings a mob of 15,000 refused to listen to either of them. Instead they shouted for George Kinloch, junior, who denounced Smith as a mere 'Corn Craik' and delighted the crowd with his call for an extension of the suffrage, the ballot, and shorter parliaments.

Popularity at the hustings, however, was no guarantee of political success where the vote was enjoyed by a privileged elite of little more than 2,000 electors. Realising that his candidature would only mean certain victory for Duncan, Kinloch withdrew in favour of Smith. All to no avail—Smith was beaten by 577 votes to 445. George Duncan continued to represent the burgh until 1857, being unopposed in 1847 and 1852, having had the good sense to disarm his critics by voting in the Commons in favour of Corn Law repeal, for pardoning the Welsh Chartists, and for an extension of the franchise.

Duncan was succeeded in 1857 by Sir John Ogilvy, who we are told, 'maintained the principle that each member for Dundee should be a more conservative Liberal than his predecessor'. Ogilvy took direct and practical interest in local affairs, serving as chairman of the Prison Board, director and chairman of the Asylum, promoting the provision of industrial schools for neglected children, and sponsoring the building of the Dundee Royal Infirmary. His one serious defect in the eyes of some of the electorate was his support for Catholic endowment in Ireland, and in 1857 he was opposed by George Armitstead on an anti-papist platform. Armitstead, who had been born in Russia and spoke little English, nevertheless polled 857 against Ogilvy's 1,092. His relative success may be explained by the hostility of many of the enfranchised in Dundee to Church establishment, a hostility which also involved the Council in the ruinously expensive Stipends Case, concerning those ministers who were financially dependent on a Hospital Fund under the control of the corporation. Ogilvy was returned unopposed in 1859 and 1865, and in the General Election of 1868, when Dundee became a two member constituency, both he and Armitstead were returned. The latter represented Dundee from 1868 to 1873, and again from 1880 to 1885.

It is clear that from the date of the Great Reform Act when Dundee first acquired its own MP, only Liberal candidates had any real chance of representing the constituency. But if the Liberal hegemony seemed to be impregnable to attack from outside, it nevertheless led to some disaffection from within. Such an internal split took place in 1873, when Armitstead stood down for a while due to ill-health, and a group of young Liberals, rebelling against the dominance of the party junta in the Cowgate, got together to promote the candidature of a complete stranger to Dundee—John Edward Jenkins.

Jenkins was a candidate of vigour, compassion and intelligence, and combined a strong imperialism (he was the founder of the Imperial Federation Movement) with a humanitarian concern for the victims of colonial exploitation (he was also agent for the Aborigines Protection Society). Jenkins stood on a Radical ticket and polled a respectable 4,010 votes against the 5,297 for James Yeaman, the Establishment's candidate in the by-election of 1873. In the General Election of the following year Yeaman again headed the poll, but by an even narrower majority, while Jenkins beat Sir John Ogilvy to take the second seat. Jenkins served until 1880, but chose not to stand in the election of that year (though oddly he did reappear briefly in 1885 as a Conservative candidate) and Dundee returned to its more accustomed moderate Liberal representation. There continued to be divisions within the Liberal camp, however, reflected in the fact that three Liberal candidates contested the 1885 election: Charles Lacaita, Gladstone's godson and a protegee of George Armitstead, Edmund Robertson, a talented London barrister who had been born at Kinnaird and who now enjoyed the support of the influential editor of the *Advertiser*, John Leng, and Andrew Moncur, a local businessman and chairman of the Texas Land and Cattle Company. Lacaita and Robertson,

Sir John Leng, local businessman and long time proprietor of the *Dundee Advertiser*, eventually agreed to stand for Parliament in 1889, when he was returned unopposed. He continued to represent the city until 1906. *Dundee Art Galleries and Museums.*

both of whom perhaps significantly were supported by the Dundee Trades Council, were returned, the latter serving until 1908, the longest term of any member in the history of Dundee.

Dundee and National Politics

While Dundee politics continued to reflect local issues and interests, they were becoming increasingly influenced by larger national and international questions. In the 1880s, Home Rule deprived the Liberals in Dundee of the support of many wealthy landowners and business magnates, some of whom, including the Baxters, decided to form the Liberal

Unionist Association. This however had little impact either on the popular vote or on the outcome of the 1886 election.

Dundee, unlike the other large Scottish towns, was never strongly Unionist. Nor were Dundee Liberals inclined to toe the party line on the Boer War too closely. John Leng, who had given in at last to long-standing pressure to stand for Parliament and had been unopposed in 1889, was not in sympathy either with militarism and the 'Great God Khaki', or with the Boers, whose government's treatment of the Uitlanders he denounced as opposed to every liberal principle. The Tariff Reform issue, however, had a more direct bearing on the local economy, and in the early years of this century, as the prospects for the jute industry were endangered by the ending of the Boer War, by the protectionist policies of America and France and by the growth of direct competition from India, some local businessmen were tempted by the thought of retaliatory action in the form of tariffs. But in the end the Free Trade traditions of the city proved too strong, and Tariff Reform was soon forgotten. In any case new forces were now at work in Dundee politics. The time was not far off when the Liberal monopoly of the city's Parliamentary representation was to be challenged and eventually overcome by Labour.

CHAPTER 12

Edwardian Dundee and the Approach of War

Dundee c. 1900–1914: Taking Stock

The final years of the Victorian era and the beginning of the Edwardian saw further changes and advances in Dundee, in addition to those which have already been mentioned. Yet it was also a period of deepening social strife and when for the first time Dundee's economic base and social conditions were subjected to close examination. While some chose to ignore the fact, there was in some circles a growing public realisation that, whatever the benefits it had brought, jute could also be a heavy weight around Dundee's neck.

During the 1880s and 1890s however civic pride abounded. The editor of the *Dundee Year Book* in 1891 was sure that 'the circumstances of life' were becoming 'brighter and happier for larger numbers of citizens'. He might have added that this was truer for the middle classes than the rest. Yet there were good reasons for his confidence. Such was Dundee's commercial and industrial reputation that in 1892 it was elevated to the rank of 'county of a city', which in legal terms placed it on a par with Edinburgh and Glasgow.

The First Improvement Act

The Improvement Act of 1871, which comprised some 20 improvement schemes, had enabled the municipal authorities, guided by the Burgh Surveyor and Engineer William Mackison, to continue with greater zeal their attempts to rescue Dundee from the worst effects of unplanned

Backlands, Overgate, early twentieth century. Dundee's overcrowded and insanitary housing conditions were amongst the worst in Scotland. The Overgate was one of the worst districts, and while criticism can now be levelled against the local authority for adopting a bulldozer rather than a more selective approach to slum clearance, the problems they faced were immense and on the whole, their actions were well-meaning. *Dundee Archive and Record Centre.*

industrial growth and begin to pull down some of the decaying and grossly overcrowded slum property in and around the town centre. Higher standards were demanded for the houses that replaced them, while building activity was such that in 1899 the *Advertiser* could confidently announce that

> 'the putting down of all new house property of the tenement class will have to stop for the best of all possible reasons—scarcity of tenants'.

In the 1870s a Working Men's Houses Association had erected ranges of concrete housing in Court St and Melrose Terrace. Indeed it was in nearby Clepington, and further east, Stobswell, as well as Polepark and Glebelands that much new building took in the later 1800s. Most though was done in the Hilltown.

In the city centre itself, streets such as Murraygate, Seagate, Commercial St and Bucklemaker Wynd (now Victoria Rd), 'about the dirtiest place imaginable in the universe' according to James Soutar, had been

Purpose-built children's play area, Magdalen Green early 1900s. Dundee was desperately overcrowded and outdoor provisions of this sort were much required. *Dundee Art Galleries and Museums*.

widened, while Whitehall St and the potentially elegant Whitehall Crescent were formed. New structures of the most 'substantial and elegant' kind arose from the rubble. One over-excited contemporary, with examples such as the Clydesdale bank at the end of High St and the Queen's Hotel in the Nethergate in mind, thought that Dundee's emerging street architecture excelled anything else in Europe. Expenditure under the terms of the 1871 Act and its two successors, of 1882 and 1892, was over half a million pounds.

Education and Social Provision: Widening the Net

In 1881, University College, Dundee, was founded, largely through the efforts of the lawyer John Boyd Baxter and funding from Miss Mary Ann Baxter of Balgavies. The inspiration had come from the establishment of Owens College, Manchester (1851), which had presaged demands in several provincial towns in Britain for university education.

The city's standing at the elementary and advanced levels of education rose too, although progress was necessarily slow in a city where so many parents expected—needed—their offspring to contribute something to the household budget, usually by doing some sort of paid work. School attendance in Dundee had been considerably below the Scottish average. The High School, until the Education Act of 1872 the sole provider of secondary education in Dundee (and the successor of the old Grammar School, Academy and English School), continued to be run privately as it had been from 1859, but the School Board, set up in 1873, opened Harris Academy in 1885 with the help of a gift of £10,000 from ex-Bailie Harris. Even though the new school offered 1,035 places, overcrowding was a problem from the outset, in the early years because its moderate fees widened the pool of potential pupils. Provision for a further 650 pupils was made in 1889 with the conversion of Morgan Hospital, opened as a boarding school for the sons of artisans and tradesmen in 1868, into a secondary school, Morgan Academy. Educational provision was widened with the opening shortly afterwards of Liff Rd School, where attendance fees were lower, and in 1908 when Stobswell Central School was opened. By 1913 the Board was employing 585 teachers.

Other improvements in public services included the building of baths in Guthrie St (1891), Constable St and Caldrum St (both 1902). These were in addition to those already in existence at West Protection Wall. Public washing houses were opened in various places. Day nurseries were also provided for the children of working women—the first in Larch St (1884).

Some attention has already been paid to the charitable work of bodies such as the Roman Catholic Church. Determined efforts were made from other directions too to provide relief for the city's poor, sick, infirm and elderly. An example is the Royal Institute for the Blind's factory on Magdalen Green (1865), another the Curr Night Refuge in West Bell St (1872), which offered temporary shelter and food to the homeless and hungry.

Help however was not given as a matter of course. One of the aims of the Dundee Charity Organisation Society (founded it appears by Sheriff Cheyne in 1886) was to 'discourage and repress mendacity', by distinguishing what the Victorians called the 'deserving' poor from 'imposters and sharpers'. Assistance was to be provided only after an applicant had been fully vetted and approved (and was not forthcoming if the destitution had resulted from drinking or illegitimacy), and even then might take the form of a ticket of introduction. Yet such was the extent of real need (and the genuine sympathy of investigating committee members) that the

Baxter Bros workers leaving Dens Works, c. 1910. The fact that many of the women were wearing hats indicates that they were weavers, who considered themselves a cut above the spinners. *University of Dundee Archives.*

Society had no alternative but to give assistance to many of the 1,000-plus cases with which their first agent, John Dunlop dealt with each year.

Impressive as all this was, it was not enough. Improvement had come late and tardily, slowed by the concern of ratepayers that their financial burden should not become overly onerous. The investigations of members of the fresh, generally young staff of University College, who had been shocked by the poverty which confronted them when they arrived in Dundee, did however provide a clear idea of the full extent of the problems which would-be reformers faced. Leading the way was the Dundee Social Union, founded in 1888. Its dynamic first Superintendent was Mary Lily Walker, one of the first female students at University College, a disciple of Octavia Hill and founder of the Grey Lodge Settlement in Dundee.

Improvement: Home Truths

As has been seen, the heady days for jute and linen had long gone. Growing competition put pressure on wage levels, which in real terms were lower in the early 1900s than they had been in 1850. The proportion of (low-paid) women to males was increasing. The suggestion, reported above, that the housing shortage had been resolved was simply a cruel illusion and a conclusion which ignored the fact that dwellings were unoccupied because thousands of women who earned 9s–12s. a week could not afford to pay the 7s.6d. which was required to rent an apartment in a good quality tenement. For this reason the market in working-class house building, which had been highly active in the 1870s, 80s and 90s as speculators sought to cash in on the shortages created by the post-1871 wave of demolition, came to a halt around 1900. And in spite of the progress which had been made under the Public Health Act of 1867 and the Improvement Acts, in 1901 one third of the citizens of Dundee still had either poor or no sanitary convenience. Although most of rebuilding of working class housing had taken place in and around the Hilltown, it was here in 1900 that most outbreaks of infectious disease occurred, although the Overgate, Blackness Rd, Middle St and Foundry Lane had unenviable records in this regard too.

Dietary habits were changing however. The evidence that more fruit, mainly apples, bananas and tomatoes, was being consumed, was encouraging. So too was the provision by some firms—J and A D Grimond at Bowbridge Works for example—of works' restaurants where well-cooked food was available. Parents of school-children or working sons and daughters however were obliged to go home to prepare meals.

One consequence of the arrival of Italians in Dundee was the appearance in the streets of ice-cream vendors, who found ready markets for their wares outside mills, as well as on Magdalen Green and in Broughty Ferry. It is questionable however whether new eating habits were for the better: nutritious oatmeal, the staple fare of rural immigrants, was widely replaced by bread and tea, especially in the households of working mothers, where there was little time for broth- and porridge-making. An alternative was to buy prepared food—soup for example—from 'cookshops'. This however was expensive, and rarely as nourishing. Fish and chip restaurants though, also run by Italians, were to become increasingly popular.

In part they were also a means of escaping from the drudgery of home life and work. So too were the city's cinemas, the first of which seems to have been the Stobswell Cinema Theatre in Morgan St, which opened its doors in 1910. Demand for temporary release from harsh reality by means of this new form of entertainment was such that two years later, in 1912, there were 13 cinemas in Dundee.

Shop assistants outside one of Wm Low & Company's stores, early twentieth century. The company is now a major supermarket chain, the headquarters of which are located in the city's Dryburgh Industrial Estate. *D. C. Thomson & Co.*

Even so, in terms of the basic necessities and material comforts, life for the majority of working class people in Edwardian Dundee was a matter simply of getting by, hanging on in a city where most family incomes were below the current poverty line. There were times however when no amount of making-do or belt-tightening would suffice, and the resources of the various relief agencies were stretched to the limit. In 1895 for instance the COS dealt with over 4,000 cases. Where possible, able-bodied unemployed men were set to work on stone-breaking, sewer construction or road-building. In some years expenditure in these areas could be considerable: in 1909–10 the City Engineer paid out £5,606 in wages on relief works. The benefits to Dundee on this occasion included the formation of Kinghorne Rd, additional sewer laying and the planting of lines of roadside trees.

Labour, Unions and Politics

Hardship, and a hardening of social attitudes which was in part due to the emergence of Labour as a political force, affected industrial relations (although it should be noted that it was often during short periods of prosperity that strikes took place and new trade unions emerged). In

Dundee as elsewhere in Britain the late nineteenth and early twentieth centuries witnessed considerable industrial militancy, amongst both skilled and 'unskilled' workers.

The Rev Henry Williamson's somewhat ineffectual Mill and Factory Operatives Union was followed during the upturn of the jute trade in 1906 by the formation of the Jute and Flax Workers Union, which owed not a little to the encouragement of the Social Union and a lot to Mary Macarthur of the Woman's Trade Union League, established in 1874 to promote women's trade unionism. As was seen in Chapter 10, there was much energy and enthusiasm amongst the jute workers to be tapped by the JFWU, which functioned initially with the hard-bargaining John Sime as president and Nicholas Marra as secretary. Male-dominated sections

John F. Sime, General Secretary (1908–1940) of the Dundee & District Union of Jute and Flax Workers. *Dundee Art Galleries & Museums.*

of the industry were represented by trade societies too, such as the Dundee and District Calender Workers' Protective Association (formed in 1887) and the Powerloom Tenters and Under Tenters Society (1911).

The appeal of trade unionism was not confined to the textile industry. By 1912 for example the Amalgamated Society of Engineers had five branches in Dundee. In the same year the Plumbing Trades Union could boast that every plumber in the city was a member. There were many more: by 1914 unions had been established in virtually every trade in Dundee. In several there were bitter strikes, by no means all of which were successful. A series of wage cuts in the shipyards in 1879, 1883 and 1884, had been resisted, but to no avail, and left a bitter legacy for the future.

One of the most notable pre-war strikes in Dundee was that of the carters and dockers in December 1912. During a series of violent disturbances several offices and works were attacked, as too were offending horse-drawn lorries, at least one of which was tipped into King William IV Dock. So serious did things look at one time that the Town Council called for the intervention of military force. Although this was not used, the services of 167 police officers drafted in temporarily from forces throughout Scotland, were.

There was in many instances a close relationship in Dundee between the trade unions, the emerging socialist groups of the period, and local politics. In 1890 for instance, Robert Bruce, president of the Trades Council, had been elected unopposed to the Town Council, while later, Labour members of the Town Council such as Alexander Wilkie and Walter Walsh, former Prohibition Party supporter and minister of the radical Gilfillan Memorial Church, played not insignificant roles in the establishment of the JFWU.

Links of this sort were useful in the women's suffrage movement in Dundee as well. One local activist, Tayport-born Agnes Husband, was a member of the School Board in Dundee, as well as the Labour Party. So too was Lila Clunas, one of the city's elementary school teachers. However, while a group of JFWU members had taken part in a suffrage procession in Dundee in 1907, and the local branch of the Women's Freedom League comprised mainly working-class women, the leadership in Dundee was almost wholly middle-class. What was a highly effective campaign in Dundee became markedly more militant during 1913 and 1914. Heckling and angry demonstrations at public meetings, window-smashing, threats and acts of arson, including the burning down of Farrington Hall, as well as the outcry which resulted from the imprisonment and forcible feeding of suffragettes in Perth prison added to the

The suffragettes in Dundee used a variety of means, both peaceful and violent, to draw attention to their cause. This cartoon, with St Mary's steeple in the background, attempts both to attack and ridicule their efforts. A branch of the Scottish League for Opposing Women's Suffrage was formed in Dundee in 1911. *Dundee District Libraries Photographic Collection.*

rising level of tension within the city which was only relieved by the outbreak of the First World War on 4 August 1914.

Hope on the Horizon: James Thomson

Yet in spite of everything, there was still an identifiable sense of optimism in pre-1914 Dundee, and a belief that the city's future could be secured and the worst of its social ills overcome without too much pain. There was not a little naïvety in some quarters; in others greater realism. The Town Council, which at long last was beginning to deal in the aggressive manner which was necessary to tackle the problems which confronted it, was a mixture of both. One of the realists was James Thomson, who in

1906 had been appointed as City Engineer and Architect. From 1910 Thomson, influenced by Patrick Geddes of University College (the 'father of modern town planning'), and the work of the Social Union, began to produce radical plans for the reconstruction of Dundee. Although his proposals were never implemented in full, many of them—albeit belatedly—did come to fruition. The most obvious is the city's ring road, the Kingsway. In short, from the search for solutions to the congested city's problems in the Edwardian era have come the principal physical outlines of modern-day Dundee.

Part III
The Modern City

CHAPTER 13

From First to Second World Wars: Dundee and Depression

Industrial Gloom

In one of the least flattering essays ever written about Dundee, the poet and Communist Hugh MacDiarmid described the city in 1934 as 'a great industrial cul-de-sac', a 'grim monument to man's inhumanity to man'. He could find 'nothing' to mask its 'utter degradation'. Another visitor in the early 1930s was James Cameron, then an aspiring journalist with D. C. Thomson, who later recalled its 'brutal melancholy' and 'singular desolation'.

There was much justification for damning descriptions like these. Jute was on its knees, struggling to catch its breath from a series of body blows: competition from Calcutta was now rampant, the produce of its mills and factories alongside the Hooghly river capable of under-cutting all but Dundee's specialist cloths; economic protectionism was the order of the day and closed off the largest remaining markets overseas; ominously too, paper and other materials were starting to replace jute for purposes for which it had long been used. Most galling of all perhaps was the knowledge that demand in the UK for jute products was rising, but that during the 1930s this was increasingly satisfied by Indian cloth, imports of which quadrupled between 1928 and 1939.

At the same time, Dundee's exports of cloth were falling off sharply. Whereas in 1900 three-quarters of the industry's output was sent overseas, in the 1930s only one-fifth left the country. The consequences were savage. Instead of profits there were losses, especially during the first half of the 1930s. Instead of expansion there was contraction, of the number of individual companies, which fell from 50 in the early 1920s to 32 in 1939, and of plant as works were either moth-balled or closed down permanently. For George Bruce, in 1935 a recently-appointed teacher at the High School, the most visible sign that something was wrong was the groups of unemployed workers standing at street corners, the 'air of depression and defeat about them' providing human testimony to the fact that at 50 per cent, unemployment in the jute trade was almost twice as high as the Scottish average.

There was not much comfort to be got in the early 1930s from looking back—or forwards. Wartime demand for sand bags had provided more or less full employment, but partly because of the nature of the product, jute had not enjoyed as fully the post-war re-stocking boom of 1919–20 which had persuaded the industry's leaders that they could view the future with equanimity. 1920 was a reasonable year for jute, but, the local Association of Jute Spinners and Manufacturers noted, this was truer for spinners than for weavers, and had not applied at all where coarser goods were concerned. By 1921 however the industry was virtually at a standstill, with most firms working only a three-day week. Normally, it was observed, the fortunes of the jute trade had fluctuated. The continuing flatness of the trade therefore was, to say the least, disconcerting, but at least profits, albeit small, were being made.

This however was to change dramatically and by 1931, after a decade of modest disappointment which ended with the onset of the worldwide Slump, one company chairman, John B Don of Don Bros, Buist & Co

Unemployed workers' march, Perth Rd, 1920s. The unemployment rate was horrendously high in Dundee between the First and Second World Wars. Marches such as this drew attention to the plight of those affected, but little action. *D. C. Thomson & Co Ltd.*

could only reflect despondently that he could not see 'a single ray of hope anywhere in the business outlook'. Yet Don's company did better than many of the others during the 1930s, partly by retreating to their original base in Forfar. Halleys, under the direction of J R L Halley during the worst period the industry had ever experienced, made losses in every year between 1931 and 1938. They were not alone.

In such circumstances, it was inevitable that labour would be shed, and it was, with the number employed in the jute industry falling from 41,000 just after the First World War to less than 28,000 on the eve of the Second. Of the city's older industries only shipbuilding saw any expansion, and even that was slight, and confined to the remarkable Caledon Company. For hundreds of those who could find nothing, resort was had to protest meetings and riots, which lasted for several days in 1921, and involved considerable damage to property both then and again in September 1931 when windows in at least 89 premises were broken, with Brook St, Hawkhill, West Port and the Hilltown being particularly badly affected. By participating in hunger marches others were able to register their criticism of a system which in the short-term at least had failed them badly.

Faint Hopes, False Starts and Dashed Dreams

However ,as has just been hinted, there were some glimmerings of hope, 'fleeting ripples of promise on a sea of despond'. Printing and publishing were expanding, with Valentines' birthday card business for example doing particularly well. D C Thomson & Co launched their first children's comic, the *Adventure* in 1920. Others followed, and in 1937 and 1938 respectively the hugely successful *Dandy* and *Beano* were launched. The merging of the *Courier* and *Advertiser* after the General Strike in 1926 heralded a new era in the local newspaper industry. Thomson's monopoly was complete, and proved able to see off any local challenges.

The food and drink trades managed to weather the storm too; indeed MacDiarmid had observed that marmalade making was 'Dundee's one flourishing industry'. Local control was lost however when the main local manufacturer, James Keillor & Son, became part of the Crosse and Blackwell group (later Nestlé, and after that Okhai) in 1918. Another major company from outside which began to develop interests in Dundee was Smedley's Ltd, who opened a raspberry canning factory in 1932. It was a pattern which was became even more pronounced in Dundee after World War II. Expansion in the food and preserve industry had further

Sugar boiling room, Lindsay & Low, Carolina Port, early 1900s. The firm made jams, bread and confectionary and was founded by William Lindsay and James Low in 1871. Low and his brother William also had a retail grocery business in Dundee. William Low began the major Dundee-based grocery chain of William Low & Co. *Dundee Art Galleries and Museums.*

beneficial effects, by for example encouraging Robert Kellie & Sons after 1918 to begin to design and manufacture equipment such as juice-filtration plants for jam and marmalade making from their East Dock St works.

Paradoxically, for most of those in regular employment the period between the Wars was one of rising real incomes. With consumer spending on the increase, department stores could hope to do well, and indeed it was in the distributive trades that most new jobs were created in Dundee, with the number of insured employees rising in the 1930s from 7,500 to 10,000. Although all of Dundee's department store concerns had been established prior to 1914, the years immediately prior to the Second World

War saw major developments within the city (although Draffen's Man's Shop had been built in 1929). These included the rebuilding and extension of the Victoria Rd premises of the long established drapery company of McGill Brothers in 1938, and in the same year, the renovation of their thriving Reform St shop by Alexander Caird & Son, a firm of men's tailors and outfitters which dated from 1879 when Alexander Caird had travelled through the Carse of Gowrie in search of his first customers. There was expansion too in the co-operative sector, notably on the part of the Dundee Eastern Co-operative Society Ltd, which had been established in 1873 but opened several new branches in the new housing schemes and outlying parts of the town between 1918 and 1939.

Indeed even within the struggling jute and engineering industries change was taking place and the challenge of the more difficult trading conditions of the 1920s and 1930s met, if late and sometimes half-heartedly. The need for a united front to deal with labour matters in general and strikes in particular, and thereafter to exercise some control over the industry's output led to the formation of the Association of Jute Spinners and Manufacturers in 1918. Inter-firm rivalries and suspicions however made it harder to achieve more positive action. 'Rationalisation' did take place, however, through an amalgamation (inspired, somewhat mysteriously, by the financier Clarence Hatry), in the form of the London-registered Jute Industries Ltd in 1920, of seven of the biggest names in jute—Cox, Walker, Sandeman, Grimond, Gilroy, Bell and Kyd.

A second textile conglomerate was in evidence from 1924, when the expanding firm of Low & Bonar acquired Baxter Bros & Co. Formed as a jute merchanting partnership in 1903 by John C Low and George Bonar, the company had first moved back into manufacturing in 1909 with the purchase of the East Port calendar. In 1913 they took over the jute weaving firm of William Fergusson & Co. The capture of Baxters however took them into the front line of the industry. Massive concerns, between them Jute Industries Ltd and Low & Bonar Ltd controlled over half of Dundee's jute trade—although several notable companies still remained outside, amongst them Caird (Dundee) Ltd, a private limited firm from 1917 following the death of Sir James Caird and his sister Mrs E G Marryat, and William Halley & Sons Ltd.

As has been seen, trading conditions were hardly propitious, yet efforts were made to improve efficiency. One way was by introducing new machinery—much of which utilised the labour of males (working day and night shifts) rather than females: indeed according to one manufacturer, the jute trade had been 'revolutionised' by 1935, with many mills having replaced their older spinning frames with high speed models. These and other modifications to working practices did nothing to improve industrial relations though, with reductions in pay rates resulting in angry disputes and not a few strikes, as occurred at Ashton Works in February 1934 when spinners were asked to attend two rather than one of the new automatic spinning frames, but for considerably less than double wages. By such means, in spinning for example, labour costs could be cut by as much as half, although at the risk of over-producing and adding to already too-high stock levels. Overwhelmingly however the reforms were achieved by adapting existing plant—the only substantial new building in the interwar period was Low & Bonar's Eagle Mills (1930).

All this and more however was unsufficient to lift Dundee's economy out of the doldrums. Even the Town Council had tried, by setting up in 1931 a New Industries Committee to co-ordinate local efforts to attract new industry to Dundee. Unashamedly, the committee commissioned a 'propaganda book', entitled *Do it at Dundee: the Story of Opportunities in No Mean City*, which extolled the advantages of the city for potential employers. Neither this nor the £70 which was paid to Electric Sky Signs Ltd to flash the 'Do it at Dundee' slogan on electric advertising boards in London and Manchester brought much in the way of tangible rewards. Much more planning, effort and state assistance was required if Dundee was to swing the operation of market forces in its favour. In 1937, a relatively good year elsewhere, unemployment in Dundee remained stubbornly high, at 22 per cent, that is twice the UK level and considerably above the Scottish average of just under 16 per cent.

Nevertheless there were areas of the city's life where the local authority could legitimately act and achieve lasting benefits. Between 1914 and 1918 James Thomson had drawn in greater detail and added to his earlier blueprint for the city's future. This had to be ambitious for as was seen near the end of the last chapter, despite the flurry of pre-1914 municipal activity major social problems remained, only to be further exacerbated by the War.

Dundee in 1918 still suffered from horrific congestion in the area centred on the High St and stretching two miles east-west and one and a half from north to south. Steps taken since the passing of the first Improvement Act had halved the death-rate in Dundee, but in the congested areas of the city the fatality rate from tuberculosis—at an average age of 37—was still disturbingly high, and had risen during the war. It was not only cramped housing and poor sanitation which was making central Dundee a dangerous place in which to live: narrow roads which had been adequate in the days of turnpikes and horse-drawn vehicles—notably those running out to Broughty ferry and along the Perth Rd—were often blocked by the thickening volume of traffic, with motor cars, lorries and buses crowding in on the tramway system which had been fully electrified since 1902. (Its peak year was 1932 when 79 tramways were in operation.) During the early 1920s however it was motor vehicles which were involved in a growing number of accidents, many of involving loss of life. Most occurred on the Perth Rd, although both the Nethergate and Lochee Rd had high accident rates too; much safer were City Rd and Rosebank St, where only three incidents were reported between 1920 and 1924.

The essential need was for wider roads within the built-up area, and for through traffic to by-pass the city centre—and in fact construction work on Thomson's plan for a broad tree-lined dual carriageway ring road, the Kingsway was well under way. The Craigiebank carriageway was also laid down. Thomson's dream of a Tay Road bridge however—for which he wanted to utilise the stumps of the fatally flawed rail bridge which had fallen in 1879—was not realised for almost half a century.

Working Class Housing: The Brave New World

Almost immediate action was taken on his housing proposals, which depended on the sort of government funding, in the form of subsidies, which the Addison Act of 1919 made available. With this, greater emphasis could be placed on house building, in contrast to pre-war programmes which had been almost wholly concentrated on slum demolition, and indeed under its provisions 710 houses were built in Dundee. Subsequent Housing Acts, of 1923 and 1924 in particular (the so-called Wheatley Act), 1930 and 1935 gave the authorities in Dundee at least part of the financial help which they required, and used to build more than 8,000 houses, plus a further 3,000-plus built by the private sector. Slum clearance got under way again too, especially after the Housing Act of 1930 which was specifically addressed to this problem, and indeed for five years during the 1930s the city's target, of 700 houses a year to alleviate slum conditions and relieve overcrowding was either met or closely approached.

The first development—the first post-war municipal housing scheme in Scotland—was at Logie. Strongly influenced by the Garden City movement, pleasantly located beneath Balgay Hill, spaciously laid-out,

Logie Housing Scheme, c.1919. Reputed to be the first council housing estate in Scotland. Although not far from the mills and factories, the wide tree-planted street contrasts sharply with the cramped and airless conditions in the central district of Dundee. Unfortunately high rents meant that those in most need could not afford to move into housing like this. *Dundee Archive and Record Centre.*

with a wide, tree-lined central avenue (off which ran appropriately named roads such as Elm St and Sycamore Place), and centrally heated low flatted blocks, Logie provided a model for others to follow. Hospitalpark, Stirling Park and Taybank did. Others failed abysmally, and the drab and monotonous tenement format predominated in numerous developments in the inner city area as in Byron St and Strathmore Ave in the mid-1920s and Maitland St, Benvie Rd, Dens Rd, Fairbairn St and the West Port in the following decade. However, even though Thomson demitted office in 1924, his management style having been found wanting, the Town Council did not entirely lose its enthusiasm for innovation where working class housing was concerned. James McLellan Brown, the City Engineer's architect from 1930, was chiefly responsible for the design of the sizeable Beechwood and Mid Craigie estates in 1934–35, which in the former case owed much to current practice in continental Europe, with open courtyards along Dronley Ave (anticipated in 1931–33 at Queen St, Broughty Ferry), sun balconies, vertical staircases (for better ventilation), and exposed brick facings. Significantly too, both schemes were north of the Kingsway. The second exodus from the city centre had begun.

In many respects then the record is impressive. While eight of the 10 local authority schemes were south of the Kingsway, the residential area of the city was spreading away from the old core, with much of the private house building of the period taking the form of uniform rows of bungalows in the west end and out towards the Kingsway. The nature and level of the state subsidies however, the stringent financial climate which prevailed between the wars and the economic circumstances of the majority of those who were most in need of being re-housed, meant that when war broke out in 1939, it was only the surface of the problem which had been scratched.

Local schisms, within the Labour Party, whose representatives on the Town Council were understandably divided between those who were content to continue building more affordable two-room dwellings and others who were anxious—as the government was after 1935—to limit overcrowding and provide greater living space, and between the local authority and D. C. Thomson, then virulently opposed to the concept of council housing, did nothing to help at a time when concerted effort was required. In 1931 15,000 families in Dundee were living in overcrowded conditions; in 1936 some 27 per cent of the city's houses were still reckoned to be inadequate in this respect. Dundee still had a higher proportion of one- and two-apartment houses than the other Scottish cities.

The basic difficulty was that local authority housing was too expensive for the typical textile worker or slum dweller (they were too often the same) in Dundee. In Logie for example, the rent for a three apartment house, not far short of £32 per annum, would have accounted for some 46 per cent of the average wage. It is hardly surprising therefore that an analysis in 1926 by the City Factor of the background of 1,560 applicants for local authority houses revealed that only 191 of them were textile workers; even fewer, 160, were labourers. Most were either skilled or white collar employees.

Even attempts to reduce building costs under the terms of the more generous (than 1923) and productive Wheatley Act, in the form of steel and concrete houses in Alpin St and Lawton Rd respectively, were insufficient to allow the Corporation to charge rents below £27 per annum—which the poorer sections of the working class could not afford. Yet some families were moved compulsorily, from the Small's Wynd and Blue Mountains area off Hawkhill for example, and rehoused where they neither wanted nor could afford to be. Despite Brown's innovative zeal in developing Beechwood, Corporation parsimony meant that the shopping units he had planned were not put in place. It was as early as 1936 that the Town Council first heard complaints from the residents of Mid Craigie not only about the absence of shopping, social and recreational facilities, but also that the expenses of getting to school and work were pressing heavily on already tight working class household budgets.

The City's People in Adversity

It would be flying in the face of the past as it really was to deny the extent to which many thousands of Dundonians suffered materially during the inter-war years, and the 1930s in particular, when the numbers on poor relief rose to an all-time high. Even the crime statistics, which show a fall in the later 1920s and early 1930s, may be indicative of the broken spirit of Dundee which observers like McDiarmid and Cameron noted. (There was however a rise in the crime rate in the second half of the decade.) Drunkenness too—cited before 1914 as the major cause of most crime in Dundee—became much less noticeable, although a drop in the figures had been observed before the First World War, as the impact of temperance campaigning, local actions such as the closing of public houses on New Year's Day (from 1891), early closing of public houses (1902 in Lochee, 1904 in the rest of Dundee) and most important of all, increases in the Spirit Duty from 1909. Yet those who were desperate, and there not a few, found solace in methylated spirits and cheap scent mixed with low grade red wine—'Red Biddy'.

The testimony of those who lived through the period, available now through the transcriptions of interviews conducted by oral historians, or the writing of people such as the millworker poet Mary Brooksbank— 'Dinna speak tae me o' the guid auld days'—confirms all this, yet it reveals too the resilience of the city's people, especially its womenfolk. There was in Dundee a tremendous capacity for enjoyment, seen for example in the popularity of the dance halls—especially the Empress, Palais, Locarno and West End Palais (and in Broughty Ferry the Chalet)— and the continued growth in the number of cinemas, 31 at one point during the 1930s if the Grand and Picture House at Broughty Ferry are included, more per head than anywhere else in the country.

They took over from the music hall and theatre, several of which, including Her Majesty's, were converted to show films, in the last case as the Majestic (1930). Only one variety theatre, the Palace, survived, providing a platform for artists such as Sir Harry Lauder and Will Fyfe. That not a single theatre for dramatic stage productions was left after 1928 is a certain pointer to where demand lay, as too was the appearance in 1936 of the sumptuous Green's Playhouse, which boasted the second largest seating capacity (4,000) of any cinema in Europe. Cox's workers who had left Camperdown at 5.30 pm, could regularly to be seen queueing outside the Astoria in Lochee before six. Diane Wood, a hand colourist with Valentines from 1932–39, wondered as she worked on pictures of Blackpool illuminations 'Where on earth wis this great place wi' a' this fun?' With the arrival of the 'talkies' and Hollywood spectaculars after 1929, she could have it, virtually anywhere in Dundee. The technology which brought Al Jolson's voice, first in 'The Singing Fool', to Dundee however had its social cost: around 100 musicians who had accompanied the previously silent movies—La Scala had an 18-piece orchestra and the King's a booming Wurlitzer organ—found themselves on the dole too.

Political Whirlwinds: Churchill, Scrymgeour and Labour

An individual who found himself rejected in Dundee was Winston Churchill, one of the city's MPs since the by-election in 1908, caused by the elevation to the House of Lords of his Liberal predecessor, Edmund, now Baron, Robertson. However, although Churchill's defeat in 1922 was humiliating and hurtful—he held to his post-defeat vow that he would never again set foot in Dundee, which earlier he had anticipated would provide him with a 'life seat' which was 'easy beyond all experience'—in the years prior to the First World War his radical brand of Liberalism was very much in tune with the perceived needs of the constituency as well as the attitude of the infant Labour Party, and in 1910 he received some 60 per cent of the popular vote, the same as Alexander Wilkie of the Shipwright's Union, Dundee's first Labour but Liberal-inclined MP who had been elected in 1906. Before the War, Churchill's most vociferous opponents were the suffragettes, whose cause, in spite of the energetic and noisy campaign waged in Dundee at the 1908 election by Emmeline Pankhurst of the Women's Social and Political Union, he attempted to disregard and consistently dismissed as being of secondary importance.

After 1918, Dundee might have gone over entirely to Labour. The city

Soldiers of the Fourth Battalion of the Black Watch departing from Tay Bridge Station in 1915. Led by Lt Col Harry Walker, a prominent local businessman, and piped and cheered on their way to the station, many of them never came back, with 235 men being killed or wounded at the Battle of Loos alone. *D. C. Thomson & Co Ltd.*

had been profoundly affected by the War, and not least by the loss of life at the Battles of Neuve Chapelle, Aubers Ridge and Loos in the summer and early autumn of 1915, during which over half of 'Dundee's Ain', the Fourth Battalion of the Black Watch, had been slaughtered. The tragic news from the battlefields, on which both officers and men perished, left a deep psychological scar on those who remained in Dundee, and who in February had cheered the troops on their way as they marched from Dudhope Castle to the West Station. Those who returned wanted something better than the social conditions they had left behind. What they found however was a city sinking inexorably into depression. Another factor which should have assisted the Labour cause was the split in the Liberal party between the supporters of the Lloyd George coalition and the former Prime Minister Herbert Asquith. In Dundee as elsewhere in Scotland the Easter Rising in Dublin in 1916 released Irish voters from their commitment to the Liberal Party and turned them in the direction of Labour.

Labour's hopes in Dundee were dashed however by the intervention

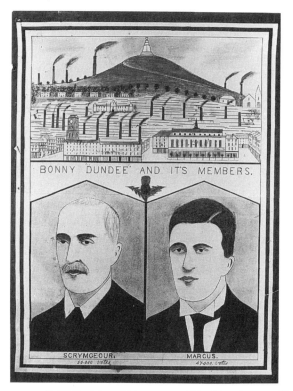

Edwin Scrymgeour, Prohibitionist candidate, won a notable victory to unseat Churchill in 1922, and secured re-election in 1923 and 1924. In 1929 he won again in association with the Labour candidate, M. Marcus, but this was to be his swansong. Defeated in 1931, he died in obscurity in 1947. *Dundee District Libraries Photographic Collection.*

of Edwin 'Neddy' Scrymgeour of the Prohibition Party. The 'stormy petrel' of Dundee's politics, Scrymgeour came from a family which had long been immersed in local political life. His father had been a Chartist supporter and worked actively amongst the poor, reclaiming outcasts and championing their cause. Before the 'Great War', Scrymgeour, an ILP member for a time but who throughout his career combined his socialism with his Christian faith, was a vociferous critic of what he judged to be an incompetent, corrupt city Corporation, of which he became an opposition member in 1905.

Although he had stood and lost at every parliamentary election in Dundee since 1908, by 1918 Scrymgeour had captured almost 28 per cent of the vote, more than Labour, and in 1922 he achieved a double victory—

election as a member for Dundee and the defeat of Churchill, about whose commitment to the city the electorate had become increasingly sceptical. Significantly, early in Scrymgeour's political career, his agent had been Robert Stewart, who between the Wars became a prominent figure in the city's Communist Party and active in demonstrations of the unemployed, referred to earlier. Immensely popular, Scrymgeour's millenial fervour and commitment to the temperance cause, as well as his uncompromising pacifism during the War (for which at first he had been vilified) and his support for adult suffrage and 'production for us instead of profit' struck a polyphonic chord with Dundee's voters, especially the newly-enfranchised women, although his successes in 1922 and 1924 also depended on tactical voting on the part of Liberal and Conservative voters who wanted to keep Labour out. They were unable however to stop the other victorious candidate, Labour's E. D. Morel, who like Scrymgeour, had adopted a tough anti-war stance. That Dundee seemed to be turning irrevocably to the left can be seen in the support for the Communist candidate, William Gallagher. Although he came bottom of the poll, he received over 5,000 votes, and double that in 1924. Scrymgeour and Labour held sway however, although after his death in 1924 Morel was replaced by Thomas Johnston, the future Labour Secretary of State for Scotland. His stay in Dundee however was cut short in 1929 when he resigned owing to a bitter dispute which had split the Trades Council and the ILP.

Throughout his parliamentary life, Scrymgeour refused to join or affiliate himself with the Labour Party, although he usually voted with them. Despite his support for Home Rule for Scotland and his passionate appeals on behalf of the unemployed, in 1931 he lost his seat to the National Government candidates. So too did M. Marcus, the Labour member who had succeeded Johnston.

With this Labour's march in Dundee was brought temporarily to a halt, strangely, as unemployment was nearing its peak (although the Communists' share of the vote did rise marginally). One of the victors was a Liberal, Dingle Foot, the other, Miss Florence Horsburgh, was both a Unionist and a woman, a double first for Dundee, which in the Victorian era had been a stronghold of Liberalism. Although Labour made substantial gains at the municipal level during the 1930s, including its first women town councillor, it was not until the 1945 General Election that the city returned to its Labour allegiance in the parliamentary arena, with the election of Thomas Cook and John Strachey. The division of the city for the 1950 election into two single-member constituencies—East and

West—made no difference as far as its political representation was concerned, although a fatal accident which cost Cook (MP for Dundee East) his life in 1952 provided a by-election opening for George Thomson, now Lord Thomson of Monifeith. With Peter Doig succeeding John Strachey as the Labour MP for Dundee West in 1963, the socialist groove in Dundee seemed deeply cut.

Dundee and the Second World War

In one sense the approach of war was more than welcome in Dundee, as demand for sandbags brought life to mills and factories which, as has been seen, had been strangely dormant for long periods in the 1920s and earlier 1930s. Even on the brink of hostilities though, in 1939, imports of raw jute were still below their pre-1914 level, and in fact unemployment continued to be higher than the national average well into the War.

Although it had been fairly clear that war was coming, Dundee, like most other British cities, was ill-prepared when it did. One of the few visible signs that preparations were being made were the sandbags piled in Court House Square and the white stripes which were being painted on pavements, lamp posts and trees in anticipation of the blackout. There were plans however—of a sort—to evacuate 24,000 women, children, expectant mothers and blind persons to towns and villages in Angus for instance. Not enough accommodation was made available however, although fortunately only 9,000 turned up to go at the appointed time. Of those, most tired quickly of the country life and returned to Dundee.

Under the terms of the Air Raid Precautions Act the Corporation had at least set up an ARP sub-committee: the problem however was that its members found it almost impossible to extract money out of the local authority purse, with one result being that Dundee had far fewer air raid shelters than would be required in the event of an enemy attack. Matters did improve though as the seriousness of the War situation was recognised, with air raid shelter provision being stepped up and various measures being taken to black out the city, such as infilling Victoria and Stobsmuir ponds and banning night-time driving up Law Hill.

As it happened, while Dundee was by no means unscathed by German raids, compared to some other Scottish towns, the city came off remarkably lightly, with fewer than 40 bombs falling within its boundaries. Only three deaths resulted from air attacks—compared to 91 in Aberdeen. The most serious raids on Dundee occurred on 4 and 5 November 1940. Indeed

Sandbags outside closes, c.1940. Although tardily, Dundee Corporation did eventually begin to take seriously the need to protect its citizens during the Second World War. As it happened, the city was little affected directly by enemy action. *Dundee Archive and Record Centre.*

it was during this brief period that the three lives just mentioned were lost; large bombs fell on the 4th, in Baxter Park and behind Taybank Works in Arbroath Rd, but no damage was done. The 5th was the worst night, and some private houses along with an electricity sub-station in the west end were destroyed, while tenement housing in Rosefield St was badly damaged. The last attack came on 22 April 1944 when a lone enemy aircraft strafed the High St during 'Salute the Soldier' week. No-one was hurt.

Although Dundee was surrounded by airfields, the city's direct contribution to the War was largely naval, and as in the First World War the harbour became an important submarine base. HMS Unicorn was used throughout as the headquarters of the Naval Officer in Charge, Dundee, while Caledon Yard was fully employed in building and repairing naval vessels. Indeed demand was so great and skilled labour in such short supply that a number of women were taken on to do work such as welding,

Bomb damage, Rosefield St, November 1940. This was one of a few occasions when Dundee was directly involved in hostilities during World War Two. *Dundee District Libraries Photographic Collection.*

which had formerly been the preserve of males. Thousands of Dundonians—many of whom never returned—served in the armed forces, in the Black Watch and the 51st Division in Egypt, Africa, Sicily and Italy.

Thus in Dundee as in the rest of Britain, the experience of 'total war' generated more powerful pressures than ever before for change—or at least for more determined action to eradicate those evils which had beset the community before 1939. There were loud calls for the demolition of slums, especially in the Overgate and Blackness, and, through new house building, of a reduction in the incidence of diseases such as pulmonary tuberculosis, which had risen during the War (as had the number of cases of diphtheria and meningitis). Above all though the demand was for something to be done about the jute industry:

> 'Dundee must not be left to the dictation of the jute bosses alone. Private and selfish interests have clearly done our city incalculable harm',

A woman heating rivets at Caledon Yard in 1942. The First and Second World Wars provided females in Dundee with new experiences of work, which after 1945 made them increasingly reluctant to go back to the jute mills and factories. *D. C. Thomson & Co.*

wrote one pamphleteer. This was unfair. Nevertheless, although the author, Alexander Annan, was a Communist, his sentiments were widely shared.

CHAPTER 14

Dundee Since the War:
Reconstructing the City

Goodbye to 'Juteopolis': c.1945–1980

Arguably, the period since the Second World War has been as momentous for Dundee as the dramatic formative decades of the early nineteenth century. Although the city retains several of its distinctive characteristics, the post-War years have seen the disappearance of most of the features which in the eyes of the outside world so scarred the face of what was one of Scotland's four great nineteenth century urban centres. A new mood can now be sensed in the self-styled 'City of Discovery'. Dundee has been visibly shaking off the dust and stour of its Victorian inheritance; its people are getting up from the floor of their former resignation.

Almost half a century has elapsed since 1945 however, and the voyage of rediscovery in Dundee has been far from smooth. Yet in contrast to the years immediately after 1918, there was considerable confidence about the future in Dundee in the late 1940s, '50s and '60s. As has been seen, wartime sacrifices had led to demands both locally and at national level that there should be no return to the conditions of the '30s, and that Dundee's housing problems and health record be tackled with much greater vigour. The city was declared a Development Area and a stream of US companies including Timex, NCR and Veeder Root occupied the advance factories alongside the Kingsway, built under the 1945 Decentralisation of Industry Act. By 1966 they were employing something like 12 per cent of the city's working population. Remarkably and in sharp contrast to the pre-War years, the jute trade found itself short of workers, and recourse once more was had to immigrant labour. The main

View looking towards Dundee during the construction of the Tay Road Bridge, which was opened in 1966. The building of a road bridge had first been proposed more than half a century earlier by the City Architect and Engineer James Thomson. *Valentine Collection, University of St Andrews Archives.*

Ninewells hospital under construction, early 1970s. Completed in 1974, it was the first completely new teaching hospital to be built in Britain, and is one of the finest hospitals in Europe. *D. C. Thomson & Co. Ltd.*

sources now however were European refugee camps—with Poles, Ukranians and Italians being the most numerous of the arrivals in the 1940s and early 1950s.

Overcrowding and housing shortages were such, even with the Temporary Accommodation Act of 1944 which had encouraged the Corporation to erect prefabricated houses, that squatters were reported to have moved in to Castleroy in 1946. New peripheral housing schemes were set down in Douglas and Angus, Camperdown and by the Scottish Special Housing Association at Mains of Fintry, and later, with greater flair, at Menzieshill, Ardler and Whitfield. Indeed under the terms of the 1950 Housing Act alone, twice as many houses were built in Dundee than in the whole of the inter-War period. This was the first assault; a second got under way after 1963, and 1968 and 1970 saw record numbers of completions of local authority housing in the city.

A new round of educational building was begun too, after a lull between the Wars, in the shape of Duncan of Jordanstone College of Art (the first design for which had been approved in 1937), Kirkton High School (1958–60) and St John's (1959–60), two of a total of 37 schools which were built in Dundee between 1945 and 1965. In 1959 the city's first tower block was completed, at the foot of Perth Rd, designed by Sir Robert Matthew for Queen's College (which University College had become, as a college of the University of St Andrews, in 1897). At around the same time the long-awaited redevelopment of the Overgate slum area was set in motion. The opening of the Tay Road Bridge in August 1966 drew Dundee more firmly into the national road network than had been possible with ferry crossings over the river. From 1967 the city could boast its own university, the University of Dundee, now independent of its older, tradition-bound chaperone. As a corollary, work was begun on Ninewells Teaching Hospital, another of Matthew's designs, and in 1968 'by far the greatest building project in Dundee since the war'. After its opening in 1974 it was to have a profound and favourable impact on health care in Dundee and beyond.

Yet by the end of the 1960s fears were being expressed that while on the whole the headlong rush to demolish and rebuild was inspired by the best of motives—to house the homeless and rid the city of its appalling congestion, it was the heart and soul as well as the congested arteries that were being cleared out of old Dundee, which had already (in 1931) lost the jewel in its architectural crown, Adam's Town House. That there was a strong smell of corruption in the air over the award of redevelopment contracts gave further cause for concern.

Doubts and Depression

Rising unemployment in the 1970s and the world economic recession of 1979–82 revealed that the city's new economic and social foundations were far from secure. Falling profits and the realisation that mechanical cash registers were now obsolete caused NCR for example to reign in their European operations and slash their employee numbers in Dundee from 6,500 to less than 1,000. During the 1970s the survival of several of the firms which formed the basis of Dundee's embryonic modern manufacturing economy depended heavily on regional aid. In short, the later 1960s and 1970s were a period of uncertainty and not a little gloom in

Ramesh Sharma, spinner at South Anchor Works in the mid-1960s. A former policeman in the Punjab, he was amongst a number of Pakistanis who came to Dundee in the 1960s and found work in the jute mills upon which the city's inhabitants were increasingly turning their backs. *Private Collection.*

Dundee's post-war history, culminating in 1979 with the *Observer* newspaper's description of the ailing city as 'a microscosm of the ills of British capitalism'.

The post-War process of change has been one of bumpy transition, metamorphosis rather than revolution. This time there was nothing like the rampant rise in population which had been so central to the making of 'Juteopolis'. Indeed after slowing considerably between the First and Second World Wars, but rising somewhat faster in the 1950s and 1960s, population growth came to a full stop in the 1970s and for the first time since the 1600s, began to fall as unemployment in the city rose. In 1991 it had fallen back as far as its 1901 level. The population mix was not static however, and as before, the city continued to attract immigrants, both from Scotland and further afield. In 1981 slightly less than one in 10 Dundonians were non-Scots. England has been the main source of 'foreign' migrants and indeed since 1841 the proportion of English men and women in Dundee has grown steadily, reaching 4½ per cent in 1981. Principally members of the professional occupational groups, they contrast with the other notable post-War migration stream, of several hundred Pakistanis, some of whom (males rather than females however) in the 1950s and 1960s were drawn in

Nursery, Dens Works, 1955. Several of the large textile firms in Dundee provided workplace nurseries for their employees' children. After the Second World war, labour was scarce and efforts were made to improve working conditions in order to attract women back into the jute mills and factories. *Private Collection.*

by the availability of employment in the once-proud Caldrum, Manhattan, Angus and Bowbridge jute works, upon which, as has been hinted, disenchanted Dundonians were at last turning their backs.

Bitter memories of unemployment, short-time working and workplace conflict in the 1930s meant that many were reluctant to return. Relocation in housing schemes far from the works made it difficult anyway. Women, who might previously have seen a period in the jute industry as their only option had had their eyes opened by their wider experiences of wartime work, and were attracted to the cleaner lighter jobs available in the new factories which lined the Kingsway, and whose managers valued their skills. Higher male earnings in Dundee made it possible for more wives to opt out of the labour market altogether, or at least pick and choose when they entered it.

Jute: Down but Not Out

Yet jute had a tenacious grip on Dundee, and indeed even at the present time (1992) two firms, Victoria Spinning (1982) Ltd and the Sidlaw Group (formerly Jute Industries Ltd) are still spinning the fibre, although only one is weaving. Several hundred people in and around Dundee continue to depend on the industry for their livelihood. In the 12 months to November 1991 over 12,000 tons of raw jute were off-loaded at the docks, from 22 ships. This of course is a small fraction of what was once brought into the port. What is remarkable however is how long jute was able to exert its influence over Dundee's economy, and even more so, on outsiders' perceptions of it.

One reason for this was that Jute Control, a legacy of the wartime need to secure the nation's jute requirements at reasonable cost, remained in force, although in a periodically modified form, until 1969, largely due to political pressures from Dundee and resulting government fears that unemployment would otherwise rise to unacceptably high levels. In effect Jute Control provided support for the industry which would otherwise have succumbed to foreign competition, although as world trade expanded again after 1945, so too did demand for jute products. As a result, the jute industry in Dundee was consuming more raw jute in the second half of the 1960s than it had been between 1946 and 1950 and indeed in the peak year of 1956 it was employing 21,000 people, compared to 13,000 at the end of the War. As late as 1966 jute remained the city's biggest single employer of labour.

For the most part however the industry's leaders had not simply sat back and basked in the shelter of their new-found protective wall. Some did, but their companies perished once it was removed. Between 1945 and 1977 the number of jute firms in Dundee fell from around 37 to 14, although this is also to be accounted for by mergers and acquisitions as the industry became concentrated in fewer, stronger hands.

Other firms used the breathing space which Jute Control gave them to embark on substantial modifications of plant, including the construction of altogether new works at Taybank and Douglasfield Mills in 1949 and 1957 respectively. New automatic machinery, costing some £11 million by the end of the 1950s, was also installed, while productivity agreements were negotiated across the industry by firms who were more inclined than ever before to professionalise their approach to labour matters. Halleys's appointment in 1947 of a Personnel Officer was one of the first moves in this direction. That the appointee was a woman (and a graduate) was an even more enlightened step in an industry which had traditionally placed only men in positions of responsibility and restricted females to

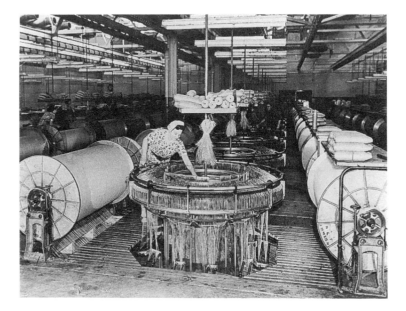

Circular power looms. These, the first in the UK, were introduced to Dundee in 1951 by Jute Industries Ltd, in Manhattan Works. The looms wove cloth tubes which were made into bags. *Dundee Art Galleries & Museums.*

subordinate roles. What is striking too is the way that firms extended their range of jute products and diversified into other areas of business activity. Into the first category comes tufted carpet backing, the major growth area as far as demand for jute was concerned in the later 1950s and 1960s, while into the latter comes Low & Bonar's move into engineering, or Halley's acquisition of a majority shareholding of Frew & Co, Ford automobile dealers. Above all though there was polypropylene.

The appearance in the mid-1960s of this new cleaner raw material, a by-product of the petroleum industry, heralded both the effective demise of jute in Dundee and the salvation of those firms which began to extrude and weave it. Led by Low & Bonar and Sidlaw Industries, who joined forces to manufacture 'Polytape', Dundee was once again well on the way to becoming a product leader. Within a single decade three firms, Sidlaw Industries, Low & Bonar and Tay Textiles (purchased in 1983 by Don & Low of Forfar) accounted for two-thirds of the UK's polypropylene output. Polypropylene silos, relatively quiet extrusion lines and rows of widely spaced and highly efficient Swiss Sulzer weaving machines replaced jute warehouses, dust-filled preparing sheds and tightly packed rows of clattering looms (although those firms which had turned to carpet backing were already using four-yard looms).

As this suggests, the industry also became highly capital intensive, and with the contraction of jute after 1966, the number of textile workers in the city fell sharply, to 8,000 in 1977. It was amongst female textile workers that the fall was steepest. In itself this was no bad thing, but not in the darkening economic gloom of the later 1970s when other opportunities were few and far between.

The Changing Face of the City

Yet gradually, over the course of the five post-1945 decades, Dundee's economic structure has become more like that of other post-industrial cities. Manufacturing employment, long the city's mainstay and its outstanding economic characteristic, has fallen to a level not far above the Scottish average of just over 20 per cent (in 1989). In common with the other cities, the growth area has been the service sector, which overtook manufacturing in 1971 and in 1981 accounted for almost two-thirds of Dundee's workforce. Increasingly, Dundee's working women, most of whom in 1911 had been in textiles, found occupations in distribution, commerce, banking and finance, education and local government. The proportion of women in the workforce however is still higher than the national average. Nevertheless, in terms of economic structure and employment Dundee no longer looks as skewed and vulnerable as it did in the past.

In housing too Dundee has managed to improve greatly on its formerly unenviable record. It is true that hurried building, low standards of design and construction and a failure to consider seriously the wider housing environment led to the need in the 1970s for a costly programme of repairs, upgrading and even partial demolition, not only in pre-War Beechwood and Mid Craigie but also the post-War schemes of Skarne and Whitfield. The multi-storey blocks which made their first appearance in Dundee at Lochee in 1960–62, and later at Whorterbank, Menzieshill, Ardler and elsewhere, are now seen by some critics as an unsatisfactory answer to the twin problems of land scarcity and the need to keep building costs to a minimum. Government financial restraints and reductions in housing subsidies in recent times have meant that rents have been rising to uncomfortably high levels. On the other hand, so much has been achieved: by 1961 the proportion of two-roomed houses had dropped to 35 per cent; by 1981, perhaps for the first time ever, there were 'more dwellings than households'. Some 4,500 were 'below tolerable standard': too many for those directly affected, but an impressively small proportion of the city's 76,374 dwellings.

CHAPTER 15

Epilogue: Towards the Rediscovery of Dundee

The 1980s: A Decade of Achievement

The depressed air which hung over Dundee at the end of the 1970s began to lift during the 1980s, although not immediately, for as was seen in Chapter 8, the city lost another link with its past in 1982 when the Caledon yard closed. Even so, this blow was unsufficiently strong to stifle more than temporarily the new-found spirit of optimism which has for more than a decade been in evidence in Dundee.

In part this has been due to the attention which has been focussed on the 'Dundee Project', which with a £24 million budget was charged by its sponsors, the Scottish Development Agency, Tayside Regional Council and Dundee District Council, with the task of preparing Dundee for its 'second industrial revolution'. Set up in 1982, it has been responsible for a series of high quality improvement programmes across the city (notably Blackness, which in 1980 had been designated Scotland's first industrial improvement area), and with the government's award to parts of Dundee 'Enterprise Zone' status, has been able to offer investors capital grants, tax holidays, rates relief, telescoped planning procedures and custom built serviced sites in six designated locations. One of these is the new Technology Park in the west end, where, most recently, General Accident have relocated their London service centre. The most spectacular (and controversial) is the Central Waterfront. Although the Waterfront plans at Riverside have failed to materialise in full, other substantial successes have been achieved, not the least of which has been the strengthening of the electronics industry in Dundee, where for example the European

Tower Building, University of Dundee, 1985. Work commenced on what was Dundee's first tower block in 1959. The flourishing University, founded in 1882, now has over 5,000 students. *Dundee Art Galleries and Museums.*

headquarters of Timex's automated teller machines division are located. In this and other sectors such as mechanical engineering, healthcare and biotechnology, the links between industry and the increasingly prestigious university, and the Dundee Institute of Technology (founded in 1887) have played crucial roles.

Achievements in business, education (including the schools in Tayside Region, whose performance in several respects now ranks amongst the best in the country) and environmental improvement have undoubtedly been important factors in Dundee's 'renaissance'. They provide only a partial explanation however. At least equally significant is the rediscovery by Dundonians of their own worth, of the uniqueness and value of their hitherto somewhat neglected and unfairly-maligned post-Restoration history.

Looking Back and Going Forwards

It is arguable that it is this which has generated much of the city's new-found confidence. The Abertay Historical Society, established in

1947 to stimulate interest in and publish local history, had played its part, but even though the Abertay recaptured something of Dundee's former reputation as a producer of formidable local histories, it appealed to a somewhat limited audience. So too did the first scholarly study devoted solely to Dundee's jute workers, William M Walker's *Juteopolis: Dundee and its Textile Workers, 1885–1923* (1979). It was however the tape-recorded investigations of the Dundee Oral History Workshop (later Project), set up in 1984 by a group of unemployed local people, which demonstrated to interviewees and a wider public that the lives and experiences of ordinary Dundonians were of real historical significance. By bringing Captain Scott's 'RRS Discovery' back to Dundee in 1986, Dundee Industrial Heritage too engendered interest and pride in local shipbuilding skills. Dundee's maritime heritage had been carefully nurtured by the Unicorn Preservation Society. The publication in 1986 of Nigel Gatherer's popular *Songs and Ballads of Dundee* revealed in print a rich song culture which had previously been in danger of being lost or confined to a restricted circle of folk-song enthusiasts.

As has been seen, serious theatre reached a low ebb during the 1930s, and was kept going only through the efforts of the Dundee Dramatic Society, which in 1936 opened the doors of the small but intimate Little Theatre, a converted jute store off Victoria Rd. Plans to establish a repertory theatre however had to wait until 1939, when the Foresters' Association hall off Ward Rd began to be used for this purpose. The Company was moderately successful during the War, although afterwards it struggled along with the city's diminishing number of cinemas (only three were left by 1981) to counter the attractions of television, which were even stronger for those living in the outlying schemes where getting to a cinema was time-consuming and costly. This was in spite of the fact that 'The Rep' managed to recruit a string of talented actors and actresses such as Ian Carmichael (1946), Glenda Jackson (1961) and Michael York (1964) who were later to become major stars of stage and screen.

Few plays however were by Scottish playwrights and the theatre-going public tended to be female and middle class. The new Repertory Theatre, opened in South Tay St in 1982, heralded a far bolder approach and was to tap new audiences with radically different productions such as Billy Kay's *They Fairly Mak Ye Work*, a hard-hitting unsentimental study of Dundee's working class past by an Ayrshire-born writer who has become one of Dundee's most ardent publicists. Due to popular demand the play had two runs in 1986, while Gordon Burnside's *A Man at Yir Back*, which was seen on its opening night in 1989 by only a third of those who wanted to be there.

As with Kay's play, Burnside's was set in Dundee, but in a modern multi-storey block, and also made full and powerful use of authentic Dundee dialect. 'Rep' performances were not confined to the new theatre building, but through its Community Theatre arm, staged on one July day in 1987 at various locations in the city, an adaption of *Witches Blood*, William Blain's well-known 'pulpy historical novel about a Dundonian family'. This took the form of a far from nostalgic, but nonetheless spectacular pageant. An integral part of both *Witches Blood* and *They Fairly Mak Ye Work* was the biting accompaniment of the music of Michael Marra, one of the figures who has been responsible for improving Dundee's somewhat uninspiring musical image, although the city did in fact produce Nat and Ron Gonnella, of jazz and fiddle music respectively, Dennis Clancy and Jimmy Deuchars, and in the pop field, the Average White Band, The Associates and Danny Wilson, and more recently, Ricky Ross of Glasgow's Deacon Blue.

In the visual arts, Dundee has recaptured something of the reputation which it had won in the later Victorian era, but later lost. This time round however the emphasis was less on patronage and more concerned with production, most notably in the case of Dundee-born Dr J McIntosh Patrick, a painter of local scenes whose work has been purchased by the Tate Gallery in London. The Painting Department of Duncan of Jordanstone College of Art too has both attracted and produced artists of outstanding ability and international acclaim, such as Alberto Morocco and former student Keith Brockie.

In the sporting arena too, Dundee has sparkled in the 1980s, although the successes of individuals such as Dick McTaggart, in amateur boxing, in the 1950s, should not be overlooked. Yet it has been in athletics and football that Dundee's status has been raised to unprecedented heights. In the former, Liz McColgan, born into a Lochee family of Irish immigrants, has become one of the world's top athletes, winning Commonwealth Gold medals in 1986 and 1990, and just failing to win at the Seoul Olympics in 1988. In football, Dundee FC has for most of present century been the city's leading professional club. In 1910 it became the first and only team from Dundee to win the Scottish Cup. In 1961–62 Dundee FC won the Scottish First Division Championship. Symbolically perhaps for a club which had in the inter-war years been financed by the profits from jute, Dundee has in the past two decades been overshadowed by the rise of its near-neighbour, Dundee United. Rooted initially in the city's Irish

Manager Jim McLean is raised shoulder high by Paul Hegarty, Richard Gough and the other members of the Dundee United football team which won the Premier League Championship in 1982–83. Their near neighbours, Dundee FC, had won the First Division just over twenty years earlier, in 1961–62. *D. C. Thomson & Co Ltd.*

community, Dundee Hibernian, as the club was known until 1923, attracted relatively small crowds and enjoyed little success until the early 1970s, since when, under the managership of Jim McLean, the 'Tannadice Terrors' have appeared in six Scottish Cup Finals (although without winning), won the League Cup (twice), the Premier League (1982–83) and gained a formidable reputation in European football—reaching the Final of the EUFA Cup in 1987.

Old Threads; New Weaves

Indisputably, Dundee in the past four or five decades has thrown off the mantle of 'Juteopolis' and lost something of the image of parochial insularity which it has with some justification been identified from later Victorian times. Yet the legacy of jute has not entirely been lost; nor have the roots been completely severed in what was initially an understandable campaign to shed the city of its dismal and often stereotyped 'Jute, Jam and Journalism' image. As has been indicated, the three are still to be found in Dundee, although in very different circumstances than they were in their hey-day. Even D C Thomson & Co, one of the city's biggest and most stable employers, has during the 1980s found that its products have lost something of their former appeal, with sales of newspapers such as *The Sunday Post* and the *Courier* falling off gently but worryingly. Sales of the *Beano* and *Dandy* however are only half of what they were at one time. In an effort to stem the tide, *The Courier* now has news rather than advertisements on its front page and uses some colour pictures. Inside though the paper still devotes several pages to reports of the minutiae of the everyday life of Dundee and the several communities it serves, and proclaims old-fashioned commonsense views which continue to make it a unique daily newspaper in Britain.

Some of the grandest and most pretentious palaces of the jute barons have gone, necessarily demolished as their structures—like the foundations upon which the industry had been built—became dangerously weak. Although almost half of the mills and factories have disappeared, fittingly, many of those which remain are taking on a new life, as the locations of new businesses, both large and small; of manufacturing activities which range from printing, through clothing to picture framing and joiners' workshops; as shops and retail outlets, as in the case of Eagle Mills; as warehouses; and as sports clubs, pubs and night clubs—Fat Sams in Lindsay St Mill for example. In the light of the appalling difficulties so many of those flax and jute workers who thronged to Dundee in the nineteenth century had in finding somewhere decent to live, it is ironic that some mills, most remarkably the monumental Tay Works, should have been converted for use as high quality flatted housing in locations which in many cases afford spectacular views over the city and the river Tay. Verdant Works has been acquired as a textile museum: in hard-headed and modest but quietly-proud Dundee, which has in the past been distrustful of casual visitors, the needs of the heritage business have been satisfied last. Belatedly, the city has discovered once again—as it did unconsciously in medieval and early modern times—that it has something worthwhile to offer the rest of the world, and that it need have no fears about opening its doors to outsiders.

It is in more than its buildings however that Dundee has managed to retain much of its individuality. In politics, where as has been seen, Dundee's electors had been capable of doing the unexpected, they again demonstrated that they were prepared to buck the trend by continuing to elect the Scottish National Party candidate, Gordon Wilson, long after the

SNP's parliamentary bubble, based on the slogan of 'It's Scotland's Oil', had burst in the mid-1970s. Only in 1987 did the Labour Party candidate in Dundee East, John McAllion, join his colleague Ernie Ross at Westminster.

And despite the process of convergence which has been taking place as Dundee fits more comfortably within the Scottish urban norm, as has been seen, manufacturing is still important, as is women's work. So too is the effect of Dundee's females on the city's culture, and the nineteenth century tradition of working-class writing, now represented amongst others by the unsentimental poetry of Ellie McDonald, who in her 'Jute Mill Sang' writes of that industry's disappearance:

Ilka day, ilka day, the hemmers
ding doun the waas o Baxters Upper Dens.

Yet, the poem continues:

Naebody ken's whit's tae be pitten in its place
naebody greets for its demise.

No tears should be shed perhaps, but the changing life and times of Dundee deserve to be better understood. This book has attempted to further that process.

Further Reading

PART I. Beginnings and Medieval Dundee

For the general background see M. Lynch, M. Spearman and G. Stell (eds): *The Scottish Medieval Town* (1988), and M. Lynch (ed): *The Early Modern Town in Scotland* (1986). On Dundee the best modern source is unquestionably E. P. D. Torrie: *Medieval Dundee: A Town and Its People* (1990); but also useful are S. G. E. Lythe: *Life and Labour in Dundee* (1958), and J. H. Baxter: *Dundee and the Reformation* (1960). Older texts such as A. C. Lamb: *Dundee, Its Quaint and Historic Buildings* (1895), and A. Maxwell: *History of Old Dundee* (1884) are well worth exploring.

PART II. Restoration to World War One

For background see two books by T. C. Smout: *A History of the Scottish People* (1967) and *A Century of the Scottish People* (1986). For Dundee industry, see B. Lenman, C. Lythe and E. Gauldie: *Dundee and Its Textile Industry 1850–1914* (1969), and for trade, B. Lenman *From Esk to Tweed* (1975) and G. Jackson with K. Kinnear: *The Trade and Shipping of Dundee, 1780–1850* (1991). Popular politics can be followed up in K. J. Logue: *Popular Disturbances in Scotland 1780–1815* (1979), and local politics in E. Gauldie: *One Artful and Ambitious Individual* (1989), a study of the career of Provost Andrew Riddoch. For social history see W. M. Walker: *Juteopolis: Dundee and its Textile Workers, 1885–1923* (1979), and E. Gordon's *Women and the Labour Movement in Scotland, 1850–1914* (1991). Immigration into Dundee is covered by J. Murray and D. Stockdale in *The Miles Tae Dundee* (1990) and women's suffrage in an essay by Leah Leneman in C. A. Whatley (ed): *The Remaking of Juteopolis: Dundee c.1891–1991* (1992). Dundee and the Second World War is the subject of A. Jeffrey's: *This Dangerous Menace: Dundee and the River Tay at War* (1991).

PART III. The Modern City

A great wealth of detail can be found in J. M. Jackson (ed) *The Third Statistical Account of Scotland, The City of Dundee* (1979), which includes an important essay on politics by D. G. Southgate. Slightly older but also wide-ranging and easier going is S. J. Jones (ed): *Dundee and District* (1968). The most recent survey is the collection of essays edited by C. A. Whatley: *The Remaking of Juteopolis* (see above). This includes studies of the economy and housing. Cultural and other aspects of the city today are dealt with in Billy Kay (ed.): *The Dundee Book: An Anthology of Living in the City* (1990). Readable studies of architecture are C. McKean and D. Walker: *Dundee: An Illustrated Introduction* (1984) and M. Watson *Jute and Flax Mills in Dundee* (1990), which is concerned with industrial buildings.

Index